I0407927

PRESSURING NORTH KOREA: EVALUATING OPTIONS

HEARING

BEFORE THE

SUBCOMMITTEE ON ASIA AND THE PACIFIC

OF THE

COMMITTEE ON FOREIGN AFFAIRS HOUSE OF REPRESENTATIVES

ONE HUNDRED FIFTEENTH CONGRESS

FIRST SESSION

MARCH 21, 2017

Serial No. 115–12

Printed for the use of the Committee on Foreign Affairs

Available via the World Wide Web: http://www.foreignaffairs.house.gov/ or
http://www.gpo.gov/fdsys/

U.S. GOVERNMENT PUBLISHING OFFICE

24–751PDF   WASHINGTON : 2017

For sale by the Superintendent of Documents, U.S. Government Publishing Office
Internet: bookstore.gpo.gov   Phone: toll free (866) 512–1800; DC area (202) 512–1800
Fax: (202) 512–2104   Mail: Stop IDCC, Washington, DC 20402–0001

COMMITTEE ON FOREIGN AFFAIRS

EDWARD R. ROYCE, California, *Chairman*

CHRISTOPHER H. SMITH, New Jersey
ILEANA ROS-LEHTINEN, Florida
DANA ROHRABACHER, California
STEVE CHABOT, Ohio
JOE WILSON, South Carolina
MICHAEL T. McCAUL, Texas
TED POE, Texas
DARRELL E. ISSA, California
TOM MARINO, Pennsylvania
JEFF DUNCAN, South Carolina
MO BROOKS, Alabama
PAUL COOK, California
SCOTT PERRY, Pennsylvania
RON DeSANTIS, Florida
MARK MEADOWS, North Carolina
TED S. YOHO, Florida
ADAM KINZINGER, Illinois
LEE M. ZELDIN, New York
DANIEL M. DONOVAN, JR., New York
F. JAMES SENSENBRENNER, JR.,
    Wisconsin
ANN WAGNER, Missouri
BRIAN J. MAST, Florida
FRANCIS ROONEY, Florida
BRIAN K. FITZPATRICK, Pennsylvania
THOMAS A. GARRETT, JR., Virginia

ELIOT L. ENGEL, New York
BRAD SHERMAN, California
GREGORY W. MEEKS, New York
ALBIO SIRES, New Jersey
GERALD E. CONNOLLY, Virginia
THEODORE E. DEUTCH, Florida
KAREN BASS, California
WILLIAM R. KEATING, Massachusetts
DAVID N. CICILLINE, Rhode Island
AMI BERA, California
LOIS FRANKEL, Florida
TULSI GABBARD, Hawaii
JOAQUIN CASTRO, Texas
ROBIN L. KELLY, Illinois
BRENDAN F. BOYLE, Pennsylvania
DINA TITUS, Nevada
NORMA J. TORRES, California
BRADLEY SCOTT SCHNEIDER, Illinois
THOMAS R. SUOZZI, New York
ADRIANO ESPAILLAT, New York
TED LIEU, California

AMY PORTER, *Chief of Staff*   THOMAS SHEEHY, *Staff Director*
JASON STEINBAUM, *Democratic Staff Director*

———

SUBCOMMITTEE ON ASIA AND THE PACIFIC

TED S. YOHO, Florida, *Chairman*

DANA ROHRABACHER, California
STEVE CHABOT, Ohio
TOM MARINO, Pennsylvania
MO BROOKS, Alabama
SCOTT PERRY, Pennsylvania
ADAM KINZINGER, Illinois
ANN WAGNER, Missouri

BRAD SHERMAN, California
AMI BERA, California
DINA TITUS, Nevada
GERALD E. CONNOLLY, Virginia
THEODORE E. DEUTCH, Florida
TULSI GABBARD, Hawaii

CONTENTS

———

Page

WITNESSES

Mr. Bruce Klingner, senior research fellow for Northeast Asia, The Heritage
  Foundation 10
Sung-Yoon Lee, Ph.D., Kim Koo-Korea Foundation professor in Korean stud-
  ies and assistant professor, The Fletcher School of Law and Diplomacy,
  Tufts University 26
Mr. Anthony Ruggiero, senior fellow, Foundation for Defense of Democracies . 38

LETTERS, STATEMENTS, ETC., SUBMITTED FOR THE HEARING

The Honorable Ted S. Yoho, a Representative in Congress from the State
  of Florida, and chairman, Subcommittee on Asia and the Pacific: Prepared
  statement 4
Mr. Bruce Klingner: Prepared statement 12
Sung-Yoon Lee, Ph.D.: Prepared statement 28
Mr. Anthony Ruggiero: Prepared statement 40

APPENDIX

Hearing notice 66
Hearing minutes 67
The Honorable Gerald E. Connolly, a Representative in Congress from the
  Commonwealth of Virginia: Prepared statement 68

PRESSURING NORTH KOREA: EVALUATING OPTIONS

TUESDAY, MARCH 21, 2017

House of Representatives,
Subcommittee on Asia and the Pacific,
Committee on Foreign Affairs,
Washington, DC.

The subcommittee met, pursuant to notice, at 2:07 p.m., in room 2172, Rayburn House Office Building, Hon. Ted Yoho (chairman of the subcommittee) presiding.

Mr. YOHO. Well, good afternoon, everyone. My thanks to my colleagues and the panel for joining me today to conduct this timely and important hearing. We are meeting today during what is probably the most significant shift in U.S. policy toward North Korea since it began its illicit nuclear program. The new administration has shown a willingness to embrace new thinking on the North Korea issue, and my goal for today's hearing is to discuss ways Congress can continue to drive a policy on North Korea that finally implements all the tools we have available.

The subcommittee will come to order. Members present will be permitted to submit written statements to be included in the official hearing record. Without objection, the hearing record will remain open for 5 calendar days to allow statements, questions, and extraneous materials for the record, subject to length, limitations, and the rules.

Again, I would like to welcome everybody here today. Secretary of State Tillerson left the world's media breathless last week when he restated that all options are on the table regarding North Korea, implying military options. His next statement that we have had many, many steps we can take before we get to that point, received less attention, but was really actually more significant.

This is what I hope to focus on today: The many unused or incompletely implemented tools that we can use before the last resort of military action, something none of us would like to see. North Korea's nuclear program has never been a bigger threat, and we need to respond with all the tools at our disposal.

If we can look at the first slide. It is a missile graph. If anything, Pyongyang has dramatically accelerated its belligerent behavior, conducting two nuclear tests and two dozen missile launches last year. Since 2015 Kim Jong Un has tested more missiles than Kim Jong Il, his father, and Kim Il Sung, his grandfather, combined, while making continued progress toward an ICBM capable of targeting nearly the entire continental U.S. If you look at the second

2

slide, you will see the range of those missiles that they currently have. While Secretary Tillerson was visiting China on Sunday, Kim Jong Un oversaw a rocket engine test that could contribute to these efforts.

For 20 years, we have responded to every North Korean provocation with either isolation or inducements to negotiate. Our efforts to isolate Pyongyang have either been incomplete or hamstrung by China. Meanwhile, North Korea has used negotiations to extract wealth without ever slowing weapons development. Since 1995, we have provided $1.3 billion in economic and humanitarian assistance to North Korea, and weapons development has only accelerated. As Secretary Tillerson stated during his trip to the region last week, this is 20 years of failed approaches.

The Obama administration's strategic patience was a low-effort strategy, taking some measures to isolate North Korea, and then simply waiting for the Kim Jong Un regime to wake up and give away his nuclear weapons. Certainly, there is plenty of blame to go around, if we are looking at George Bush taking North Korea off the State Sponsors of Terrorism record, or the Clinton administration allowing North Korea to even start a nuclear program, although it was deemed for peaceful purposes, we saw they strayed from that.

This ineffective approach has gotten us no closer to a denuclearized peninsula. A more forward leaning North Korea policy will require more effort and resolve, as we have seen passivity fail time and again. It takes time. It takes time for these threats—and take the threat seriously and use our entire toolbox.

Congress can be important in this work, and we have to ensure that the things that we set forward, we follow through on. We have to ensure continued robust support for injecting outside information into North Korea to encourage defection and expose Kim's propaganda. Thae Yong-Ho, the highest ranking North Korean defector in decades, recently said this was the best way to force change in North Korea.

This committee has also done important work in increasing financial pressure on the regime, and I look forward to continuing our work on the sanctions this Congress.

We should also re-list North Korea as a State Sponsor of Terrorism in light of its long history of horrific crimes, most recently, the assassination of Kim Jong Nam with the VX nerve agent in Malaysia.

The administration must also start using its secondary sanctions authority against the Chinese entities that have allowed for North Korea's continued weapons development. China accounts for 90 percent of North Korea's economic activity. The failed policies of the past assumed that if the United States did not anger China, China would help promote de-nuclearization. It is time to stop pretending that China's North Korea policy is motivated by anything else than extreme self-interest of China. China has benefited from undermining sanctions and tolerating North Korea's nuclear belligerence. North Korea's missiles are not aimed at China, and the growing security challenge is an excellent distraction from China's own illicit activities.

I have been heartened to see both Secretary Mattis and Tillerson reaffirm our critical alliance with the Republic of Korea and Japan. Our officials also rightly continue to reject proposals that we halt military exercise with South Korea to bring North Korea to negotiations.

China's retaliation against South Korea over the deployment of THAAD is also unacceptable. THAAD is solely oriented toward the defense of South Korea. China should address the threat that makes that necessary rather than interfering with our security cooperation.

It is encouraging to hear that the administration will not make further concessions to hold talks or to negotiate a weapons freeze that leaves North Korea's threat in place. SWIFT's recent decision to finally cut off the remaining North Korean banks from its financial messaging service has also been a welcome development.

I am looking forward to help build a stronger, more complete North Korea policy, and look forward to hearing from our panel on these developments and options. Without objections, the witnesses' written statements will be entered into the hearing.

I now turn to the ranking member for any remarks he may have.

[The prepared statement of Mr. Yoho follows:]

Pressuring North Korea: Evaluating Options
Subcommittee on Asia and the Pacific
House Committee on Foreign Affairs
Tuesday, March 21, 2017, 2:00 p.m.
Opening Statement of Chairman Ted Yoho

Good afternoon everyone, and my thanks to my colleagues and the panel for joining me today to conduct this timely and important hearing. We're meeting today during what is probably the most significant shift in U.S. policy towards North Korea since it began its illicit nuclear program. The new administration has shown a willingness to embrace new thinking on the North Korea issue, and my goal for today's hearing is to discuss ways Congress can continue to drive a policy on North Korea that finally implements all the tools we have available.

Secretary of State Tillerson left the world's media breathless last week when he restated that "all options are on the table" regarding North Korea, implying military options. His next statement, that "we have many, many steps we can take before we get to that point," received less attention but was actually more significant.

This is what I hope to focus on today: the many unused or incompletely implemented tools we can use before the last resort of military action, something none of us would like to see. North Korea's nuclear program has never been a bigger threat, and we need to respond with all the tools at our disposal.

If anything, Pyongyang has dramatically accelerated its belligerent behavior, conducting two nuclear tests and two dozen missile launches last year. Since 2015, Kim has tested more missiles than Kim Jong Il and Kim Il Sung combined, while making continued progress towards an ICBM capable of targeting nearly the entire continental U.S. While Secretary Tillerson was visiting China on Saturday, Kim Jong Un oversaw a rocket engine test that could contribute to these efforts.

For 20 years, we have responded to every North Korean provocation with either isolation or inducements to negotiate. Our efforts to isolate Pyongyang have either been incomplete, or hamstrung by China. Meanwhile, North Korea has used negotiations to extract wealth without ever slowing weapons development.

Since 1995, we have provided $1.3 billion in economic and humanitarian assistance to North Korea, and weapons development has only accelerated. As Secretary Tillerson stated during his trip to the region last week, this is "20 years of a failed approach."

The Obama administration's "strategic patience" was a low-effort strategy, taking some half-measures to isolate North Korea, and then simply waiting for Kim Jong Un to wake up and give away his nuclear weapons.

This ineffective approach has gotten us no closer to a denuclearized peninsula. A more forward-leaning North Korea policy will require more effort and resolve, as we've seen passivity fail time and again.

It's time to take this threat seriously and use our entire toolbox. Congress can be an important part of this work. We have to ensure continued, robust support for injecting outside information into North Korea to encourage defection and expose Kim's propaganda. Thae Yong-ho, the highest ranking North Korean defector in decades, recently said that this was the best way to force change in North Korea.

This Committee has also done important work in increasing financial pressure on the regime, and I look forward to continuing our work on sanctions this Congress. We should also relist North Korea as a state sponsor of terror in light of its long history of horrific crimes, most recently the assassination of Kim Jong Nam with VX nerve gas.

The administration must also start using its secondary sanctions authority against Chinese entities that have allowed for North Korea's continued weapons development. China accounts for 90 percent of North Korea's economic activity. The failed policies of the past assumed that if the United States did not anger China, it would help promote denuclearization.

It's time to stop pretending that China's North Korea policy is motivated by anything other than extreme self-interest. China has benefitted from undermining sanctions and tolerating North Korea's nuclear belligerence. North Korea's missiles are not aimed at China, and the growing security challenge is an excellent distraction from China's own illicit activities.

I've been heartened to see both Secretary Mattis and Secretary Tillerson reaffirm our critical alliances with the Republic of Korea and Japan. Our officials also rightly continue to reject China's proposal that we halt military exercises with South Korea to bring North Korea to negotiations.

China's retaliation against South Korea over the deployment of THAAD is also unacceptable. THAAD is solely oriented towards the defense of South Korea. China should address the threat that makes it necessary, rather than interfering with our security cooperation.

It's encouraging to hear that the administration will not make further concessions to hold talks, or negotiate a weapons freeze that leaves the North Korean threat in place. SWIFT's recent decision to finally cut off the remaining North Korean banks from its financial messaging service has also been a welcome development.

I'm looking forward to helping build a stronger, more complete North Korea policy, and look forward to hearing from our panel on these developments and options.

Mr. SHERMAN. Thank you, Chairman Yoho. I want to thank you for holding these hearings in light of North Korea testing of missiles in March and February of this year, with missiles landing in Japan's exclusive economic zone. I join with you in believing that, certainly, North Korea ought to be listed as a State Sponsor of Terrorism, not only because its actions threaten the United States, but because of the assassination in Malaysia and the continuing terrorism, having kidnapped Japanese civilians and held them to this day. It is not an act of terrorism just when you do the kidnapping; it is an act of terrorism every day you hold the victim, or perhaps, in some cases, the body of the victim if they have expired.

The last time we held this hearing was just a few months ago in September. North Korea had just conducted its fifth and largest nuclear weapons test. Kim Jong Un's intentions are clear: He wants to be able to be accepted as a world nuclear power capable of threatening the United States.

A February 27 report from the U.N. Panel of Experts on North Korea to the U.N. Security Council detailed the regime's flouting of sanctions by trading in prohibited goods and by using evasion techniques. The Panel of Experts' report also highlighted that North Korean banks, including designated banks or correspondent or pay-through accounts with foreign banks, foreign joint ventures with foreign companies maintain representative offices abroad, and that trading companies linked to North Korea, including designated entities, open bank accounts that perform the same financial services as banks.

All of these issues need to be addressed, but we need to approach the problem of North Korea with both a clinched fist and an open hand. Our Secretary of State says all options are on the table. I don't think the military option is on the table. I think, to some extent, his statement distracts us from the actions that we really need to take, actions that Wall Street will not like. At the same time, we need to put all options on the table in terms of the concessions that we are willing to make, or reasonable concessions, at least, in order to secure a binding and verifiable freeze and rollback of North Korea's nuclear missile programs.

We need our partners and allies. Whatever government emerges in South Korea should not reopen the Kaesong plant, because when North Korea can sell slave labor, whether it does so on the Korean Peninsula or in Malaysia, where there are 1,000, I guess they don't call them slaves, but indentured workers, whose earnings go to Kim Jong Un, when that happens, not only do we violate labor standards, but we enrich the regime.

As to China, our efforts have not been enough to change China's cooperation with North Korea. China accounts for 90 percent of North Korea's legitimate trade, 95 percent of its foreign direct investment. It is North Korea's lifeline. China recently cut off purchases of North Korean coal. There is more there than meets the eye. China may have already reached its quota under U.N. Security Council resolution, which limits the amount of coal that it can purchase in any year.

China fully understands what is the Wall Street policy here: Make a lot of noise, pound the table, sanction a few companies, but don't interrupt the huge exports of China to the United States; do nothing that really forces China to change its policy, but pound the table loud enough so that you cannot be accused of being weak.

Strength is not proven by volume. Strength is proven by success. We are not going to be successful in changing China's policy until we are willing to put a tariff on all Chinese, or virtually all Chinese, exports to the United States. Wall Street doesn't want us to do it, therefore, we won't do it. Therefore, the real objective of the Trump administration is to yell loudly, call that strength, and not actually do anything that would upset Wall Street or be effective. One more area I think we can be effective is in deterring Pyongyang from selling nuclear missile material or completed weapons to terrorist organizations or to Iran. This starts with reaching an agreement with China that at least they should not allow overflights of their territory from Iran to Pyongyang, unless those flights stop for inspection or refueling, which would include inspection, in China. If China is allowing planes to connect Iran and North Korea, cash can be going in one direction, missile material in the other, and China has to be held responsible.

The North Korean Human Rights Act is set to expire. We need to reauthorize it this year.

Yes, we have had 20 years of failure, 20 years in which we have refused to make any concession, not even a nonaggression pact, and therefore, we can seem strong while accomplishing nothing. I suspect that that is the policy that we will continue, and that we will be back in this room next year and the year after, and the only difference is the latest North Korean provocation will be a missile that flew further or a nuclear stockpile that is larger. I regret that I believe we will be in this room within a few years to talk about not atomic, but hydrogen nuclear weapons.

Mr. YOHO. Let's hope not. And that is the purpose of this meeting, so that we can help draft those.

Mr. SHERMAN. I hope so. I yield back.

Mr. YOHO. We are going to go now to members. We each get a minute, and we are going to hold you to that so that we can get on with that. We first go to Dana Rohrabacher.

Mr. ROHRABACHER. Okay. It is time to get tough with Korea, right? North Korea, however, shouldn't be mistaken, when we get tough with North Korea, that we are getting tough with the North Korean people. North Korean people are subjugated people. They are kept in place by a bloody tyranny. And whatever we do, it should be aimed at the leadership in North Korea, and not the people of North Korea.

So, in fact, we should look at the people of North Korea as potential allies, our greatest potential allies in bringing about what needs to be brought about to have a more peaceful and secure world. Our goal should be the removal of this wacko regime that is just—that now is threatening the world as it develops its nuclear capability. Let us not forget that the Chinese have had the most influence of anyone. They could have stopped this a long time ago.

So I suggest we look at banking, I suggest we look at other ways of putting the pressure directly on the North Korean leadership and make sure that our Chinese friends know they are accountable for what happens.

Mr. YOHO. Thank you, Mr. Rohrabacher. We are going to go to another Californian, Dr. Ami Bera.

Mr. BERA. Thank you, Mr. Chairman. Thanks for having this hearing.

Obviously, the North Korean dilemma isn't one administration or another administration. As complicated as it was in the Obama administration, it is probably a bit more complicated now as they continue to move forward.

I think the first step is to reassure our allies in the region, the Republic of Korea and Japan, that our commitment to the region, our commitment to the defense of the region has not wavered. I think that is important for the North Koreans to understand we are not wavering in our commitment.

I do look forward to the testimony of the witnesses. I look forward to how we move forward, but, again, provocation on North Korea's part is not a way to start a dialogue or start a path toward de-nuclearization or stability on the peninsula. This starts with dialogue and standing down. Again, our commitment is unwavering.

I will yield back.

Mr. YOHO. Thank you, Doctor. We will next go to Steve Chabot from Ohio.

Mr. CHABOT. Thank you, Mr. Chairman. Thanks for holding this hearing.

Days ago, North Korea touted the successful test of its new high thrust rocket engine. If this test was, in fact, successful, it would underscore North Korea's growing nuclear delivery capabilities. Unfortunately, this does not come as a surprise, considering the rogue state's relentless pursuit of nuclear armament.

I am deeply concerned that this test confirms, yet again, that North Korea is making significant advances in its nuclear weapon technology. Other reports indicate that North Korea continues to make technological advancements in its delivery systems, and that it will soon be able to strike the United States.

Now, considering the uncertainty of the political situation in South Korea and our new leadership here in the United States, it is important that Congress and the new Trump administration work together to come up with a coherent strategy.

Let there be no mistake: If North Korea attains the ability to reach American soil with a nuclear device, our Government will have failed the American people.

I yield back.

Mr. YOHO. Thank you, sir. We will next go to Ms. Tulsi Gabbard from the State of Hawaii.

Ms. GABBARD. Thank you very much, Mr. Chairman. Thank you, gentlemen, for being here.

I represent a State that falls directly within North Korea's range of their current intercontinental ballistic missile capabilities, and obviously, the people of my district in Hawaii view North Korea's increased capabilities as a direct threat to the people of our State, as it is a direct threat to our country.

Obviously, the current strategy that has been deployed for so long toward North Korea has been ineffective, both in achieving a de-nuclearized North Korea, but also in putting a halt on their ever-increasing capabilities. This is something that we hear often by those who come and speak to us, a clear identification of the problem and the imminent threat it poses, but very few people have constructive solutions. So I am looking forward to hearing your comments, and hope that you can offer some ideas on how our current strategy should be changed. Thank you.

Mr. YOHO. I appreciate your words. Next, we will go to Mrs. Ann Wagner from Missouri.

Mrs. WAGNER. Thank you, Mr. Chairman.

With a new administration in the White House, and South Korean Presidential elections scheduled for May, figuring out how the new U.S. and ROK administrations can act as harmoniously as possible in addressing the North Korean threat is certainly the question of the hour.

Recently, former Director of National Intelligence James Clapper said that convincing North Korea to give up its nuclear arms is a "lost cause." But the Obama administration's policies of strategic patience that have allowed the Kim regime to prosper is now over. And as has been stated here earlier, Secretary Tillerson says that all options are back on the table.

Whether we can roll back the damage of the international failure to temper the Kim regime depends largely on whether we choose to understand North Korea's intentions, and develop an intelligible strategy in response. I look forward to hearing your testimonies and engaging on this issue.

And I thank you, Mr. Chairman.

Mr. YOHO. We thank you.

Next, we are going to go to our witnesses today, but before we start, Mr. Klingner, I had the opportunity to sit with you the other day. And, you know, I feel very strongly about that, that the information we will hear from you guys today will go into policies that we are going to direct at the State Department, to the White House, so that as my ranking member here, Mr. Sherman, said, we don't have to have this talk again. I know you guys are tired of having the talk over and over again. So we want to have very concise language that we can take, and go to the administration to redirect this foreign policy so that we can bring the threat of the nuclear weapons—take it away.

So, we are thankful today to be joined by Mr. Bruce Klingner, senior research fellow for Northeast Asia at the Heritage Foundation; Dr. Sung-Yoon Lee, Kim Koo-Korea Foundation professor in Korean studies and assistant professor at Tufts University, The Fletcher Law School and Diplomacy; and Mr. Anthony Ruggiero, senior fellow at the Foundation for Defense of Democracies.

We thank the panel for joining us today to share their experience and your expertise, and I look forward to your comments. We are going to—if you would, stay with the timer, 5 minutes, don't forget to push the talk button. And you will hear me kind of rattle the gavel little bit if you go over that. We look forward to getting onto the questions.

So, Mr. Klingner, if you would start. Thank you.

STATEMENT OF MR. BRUCE KLINGNER, SENIOR RESEARCH FELLOW FOR NORTHEAST ASIA, THE HERITAGE FOUNDATION

Mr. KLINGNER. Thank you, Chairman Yoho, Ranking Member Sherman, and distinguished members of the panel. It is truly an honor to be asked to appear before you again.

The security situation on the Korean Peninsula is dire and worsening. There is a disturbingly long list of reasons to be pessimistic about maintaining peace and stability in Northeast Asia.

In response, some experts advocate negotiating a nuclear freeze, but a premature return to talks would be another case of "abandon hope, all ye who enter here." Would the ninth time be the charm? Pyongyang signed four previous agreements never to develop nuclear weapons, and once caught with their hand in the nuclear cookie jar, four subsequent promises to abandon those weapons. And a record of 0-for-8 does not instill a strong sense of confidence about any future attempts of negotiation.

During the decades of negotiation, the U.S. and its allies offered economic benefits, developmental and humanitarian assistance, diplomatic recognition, declarations of nonhostility, and turning a blind eye to violations and nonimplementation of U.S. law. All failed. Seoul has signed 240 inter-Korean agreements and participated in large joint economic ventures at Kaesong and Kumgangsan. All of these failed to induce Pyongyang to begin to comply with its de-nuclearization pledges, moderate its belligerent behavior, or implement economic or political reform.

Moreover, it is difficult to have dialogue with a country that shuns it. It was North Korea that closed the New York Channel in July 2016, severing the last official communication link; they walked away from inter-Korean dialogue; and even refuses to answer the phone in the Joint Security Area which straddles the DMZ.

And the freeze proposals all call for yet more concessions by the U.S. and its allies in return for North Korea to begin—to undertake a portion of what it has already obligated to do under U.N. resolutions. The strongest case against diplomacy can be found in the regime's own words, in which the highest levels of the regime, including Kim Jong Un, have repeatedly and unambiguously made clear they will never abandon their "treasured sword" of nuclear weapons, as well as that the Six-Party Talks are dead and "null and void." Hope is a poor reason to ignore a consistent track record of failure.

And there are consequences of a bad agreement. A freeze would undermine the nonproliferation treaty and send the wrong signal to nuclear aspirants like Iran, that the path is open to nuclear weapons. Doing so would sacrifice one arms control agreement on the altar of expediency to get another.

Instead, there is now an international consensus on the need to punish and pressure North Korea for its repeated violations. Increased financial sanctions, combined with the increasing pariah status of the regime from its human rights violations, have led nations and companies to sever their business relationships with North Korea, curtail North Korean overseas workers visas, and reduce the flow of hard currency to the regime. I have included a lengthy list of these actions in my written testimony.

Cumulatively, these efforts reduce North Korea's foreign revenue sources, they increase strains on the regime, and generate internal pressure. North Korean overseas financial operations are suffering.

The U.S. has had all the authorities it needs. It has just lacked the political will to go beyond timid incrementalism in enforcing our laws.

Now is also the time to break some China. The U.S. should stop pulling its punches, and go where the evidence takes it. The North Korea Sanctions and Policy Enhancement Act mandates secondary sanctions on third country, including China, whose banks and companies that violate U.N. sanctions and U.S. laws.

Other measures that I will mention just briefly, but cover in more depth in my written testimony are, as you have already pointed out, put North Korea back on the State Sponsors of Terrorism list. Since its removal from the list, Pyongyang has conducted numerous terrorist acts which meet the U.S. legal requirements for being put back on the list. Returning North Korea to the list would be a proper and pragmatic recognition of the behavior that violates U.S. statutes. It also increases North Korea's diplomatic and economic isolation for its actions.

Also, we should designate additional entities for human rights abuses. Last year, the U.S. finally imposed sanctions on North Korean leader Kim Jong Un and 15 other entities for their ties to North Korea's atrocious human rights records, which constitute crimes against humanity.

Also, we should improve information access into North Korea. Promoting democracy and access to information in North Korea is in both the strategic and humanitarian interests of the United States. International efforts to penetrate the information firewall in North Korea should expand on ongoing efforts with radios, DVDs, cell phones, and thumb drives, but also utilize new technology for more innovative ways to get information in and out of North Korea.

In conclusion, Washington must sharpen the choice for North Korea by raising the risk and the costs for its actions, as well as for those, particularly Beijing, who have been willing to facilitate the regime's prohibited programs and illicit activities and condone its human rights violations.

Sanctions require time and political will to maintain them in order to work. We must approach sanctions pressures and isolation in a sustained and comprehensive way. It is a policy of a slow python constriction rather than a rapid cobra strike.

Thank you, again, for the privilege of appearing before you.

[The prepared statement of Mr. Klingner follows:]

The
Heritage Foundation

CONGRESSIONAL TESTIMONY

Sisyphean Diplomacy: The Dangers of Premature Negotiations with North Korea

Testimony before the

House Committee on Foreign Affairs

Subcommittee on Asia and the Pacific

March 21, 2017 - Pressuring North Korea: Evaluating Options

Bruce Klingner

Senior Research Fellow, Northeast Asia

The Heritage Foundation

214 Massachusetts Avenue, NE • Washington, DC 20002 • (202) 546-4400 • heritage.org

13

My name is Bruce Klingner. I am the Senior Research Fellow for Northeast Asia at The Heritage Foundation. The views I express in this testimony are my own, and should not be construed as representing any official position of The Heritage Foundation.

The security situation on the Korean Peninsula is dire and worsening. There is a disturbingly long list of reasons to be pessimistic about maintaining peace and stability in northeast Asia.

- North Korea's growing nuclear and missile capabilities are already an existential threat to South Korea and Japan and will soon be a direct threat to the continental United States. Pyongyang's decades long quest for an unambiguous ability to target the United States with a nuclear-tipped ICBM may be entering endgame.
- Pyongyang undertook a robust nuclear and missile test program in 2016, achieving several breakthroughs, expanding its threat to our allies and U.S. troops in the region. Recent missile launches shows Pyongyang will continue its provocative behavior under the Trump Administration.
- Kim Jong-un declared the regime has "reached the final stage of preparations to test-launch an intercontinental ballistic missile" and would continue to build up "the capability for preemptive strike." Pyongyang declared "The ICBM will be launched anytime and anywhere."
- Pyongyang has repeatedly vowed it will never abandon its nuclear arsenal and dismissed the potential for denuclearization negotiations.
- China reacted viscerally to the allied deployment of the THAAD ballistic missile defense system. Beijing has repeatedly shown it is more willing to punish defense responses than the threatening behavior that precipitated them.
- North Korea used VX – a chemical weapon of mass destruction – to assassinate the half-brother of Kim Jong-un in a crowded civilian airport.
- U.S. policymakers, lawmakers, and experts assess that the time for dialogue with Kim Jong-un has passed and that the U.S. must impose augmented sanctions to tighten the economic noose on North Korea. Though it is the proper policy, it carries the risk of strong reactions by Pyongyang and Beijing.
- There is growing concern in South Korea about U.S. capabilities, resolve, and willingness to defend their country, particularly once North Korea demonstrates an unambiguous ability to threaten the U.S. mainland with nuclear weapons.
- The impeachment of Park Geun-hye will bring a liberal successor who may pursue policies at odds with U.S. objectives.
- There is growing advocacy for preemptive military actions against North Korea, mimicking regime comments of its own preemption plans. This raises the risk of military conflict, either intentionally or through miscalculation.

Negotiations with North Korea: Abandon hope all ye who enter here

As the Trump Administration conducts its North Korea policy review, it faces a perfect storm of Asian headaches, threats, and crises. Initial indications are that the administration will emphasize improving defense capabilities, particularly ballistic missile defense; augmenting pressure tactics on the regime; and seeking ways to get Beijing to fully enforce UN sanctions.

While the door will remain open for diplomatic engagement, it will likely only be a secondary objective due to North Korea's recent provocative behavior and the international consensus to pressure the regime for its repeated violations of UN resolutions and international laws.

Advocates for engagement will insist that the only way to constrain Pyongyang's growing nuclear arsenal is to rush back to nuclear talks without insisting on preconditions. But there is little utility to such negotiations as long as Pyongyang rejects their core premise, which is abandonment of its nuclear weapons and programs.

Ninth time the charm? Promoting another attempt at a negotiated settlement of the North Korean nuclear problem flies in the face of the collapse of Pyongyang's previous pledges never to develop nuclear weapons or, once caught with their hand in the nuclear cookie jar, subsequent promises to abandon those weapons.

Pyongyang previously acceded to the 1992 North–South Denuclearization Agreement, the Non-Proliferation Treaty, the International Atomic Energy Agency (IAEA) safeguards, the Agreed Framework, three agreements under the Six-Party Talks and the Leap Day Agreement – all of which ultimately failed. A record of zero for eight does not instill a strong sense of confidence about any future attempts.

For over 20 years, there have been official two-party talks, three-party talks, four-party talks and six-party talks to resolve the North Korean nuclear issue. The U.S. dispatched government envoys on numerous occasions for bilateral discussions with North Korean counterparts. The U.S. and its allies offered economic benefits, developmental assistance, humanitarian assistance, diplomatic recognition, declaration of non-hostility, turning a blind eye to violations and non-implementation of U.S. laws.

Seoul signed 240 inter-Korean agreements on a wide range of issues and participated in large joint economic ventures with North Korea at Kaesong and Kumgangsan. Successive South Korean administrations, including those of conservative Presidents Lee Myung-bak and Park Geun-hye, offered extensive economic and diplomatic inducements in return for Pyongyang *beginning* to comply with its denuclearization pledges.

There have been extensive unofficial outreach efforts through visits by philharmonic orchestras, soccer teams, Olympic teams, cheerleading teams and so on. Yet, all of these official and unofficial initiatives failed to induce political and economic reform or moderate North Korea's belligerent behavior.

It is also difficult to have a dialogue with a country that shuns it. North Korea closed the "New York channel" in July 2016, severing the last official communication link. Pyongyang walked away from senior-level meetings with South Korean counterparts in December 2015, precipitating the collapse of inter-Korean dialogue. In the Joint Security Area on the Demilitarized Zone (DMZ), North Korea refuses to even answer the phone or check its mailbox for messages from the U.S. and South Korea.

Hope springs eternal. Despite these failures, there has been a renewed advocacy by some experts to negotiate a nuclear freeze. The proposals all share a common theme in calling for yet more concessions by the U.S. to encourage Pyongyang to come back to the negotiating table in return for a commitment by the North to undertake a portion what it is already obligated to do under numerous UN resolutions.

Been There, Done That. A nuclear freeze was already negotiated with the February 2012 Leap Day Agreement in which the U.S. offered 240,000 tons of nutritional assistance and a written declaration of no hostile intent. In return, North Korea pledged to freeze nuclear reprocessing and enrichment activity at the Yongbyon nuclear facility, not to conduct any nuclear or missile tests and to allow the return of International Atomic Energy Association inspectors to Yongbyon.

That agreement crashed and burned within weeks. Indeed, all eight denuclearization agreements with North Korea were variants on a nuclear freeze. Yet that does not seem to deter freeze proponents from advocating another try. Hope is a poor reason to ignore a consistent track record of failure.

North Korea Not Interested in Denuclearization. Nuclear freeze proponents have provided no rationale for why yet another attempt at negotiations would be any more successful than previous failures. Nor have they provided any evidence indicating a North Korean policy shift away from its declared rejection of denuclearization.

Indeed, the strongest case against diplomacy can be found in the regime's own words, in which the highest levels of the regime, including Kim Jong Un, have repeatedly and unambiguously made clear that Pyongyang will never abandon the "treasured sword" of its nuclear arsenal and that the Six-Party Talks are "null and void."

Pyongyang has indicated that no level of economic benefits could address the security concerns that the regime cites as justification for its nuclear programs. As such, there is no utility in offering such assistance. Indeed, opening North Korea to outside economic assistance is an anathema to the regime since it allows the contagion of outside influence to reach the populace.

Similarly, since North Korean nuclear weapons are purported to be a response to the "hostile policy" of the U.S., then no South Korean offers of economic assistance or security measures could dissuade Pyongyang from its nuclear programs.

Too High a Price. What would the U.S. and its allies have to offer to achieve a freeze? Those things that were previously offered to no effect? Or would Washington and others have to provide even greater concessions and benefits? The regime has an insatiable list of demands, which include:
- **Military demands** – the end of U.S.-South Korean military exercises, removal of U.S. troops from South Korea, abrogation of the bilateral defense alliance between the U.S. and South Korea, cancelling of the U.S. extended deterrence guarantee, postponement or cancellation of the deployment of THAAD to South Korea and worldwide dismantlement of all U.S. nuclear weapons;
- **Political demands** – establishment of formal diplomatic relations with the U.S. signing of a peace treaty to end the Korean War, and no action on the UN Commission of

Inquiry report on North Korean human rights abuses;
- **Law enforcement demands** – removal of all UN sanctions, U.S. sanctions, EU sanctions and targeted financial measures; and
- **Social demands** against South Korean constitutionally protected freedom of speech (pamphlets, "insulting" articles by South Korean media, and anti–North Korean public demonstrations on the streets of Seoul).

Consequences of a bad agreement. A freeze would be a *de facto* recognition and acceptance of North Korea as a nuclear weapons state. Doing so would undermine the Non-Proliferation Treaty and send the wrong signal to other nuclear aspirants that the path is open to nuclear weapons. Doing so would sacrifice one arms control agreement on the altar of expediency to get another.

A nuclear freeze agreement without verification would be worthless. North Korea's grudging admission of its prohibited highly enriched uranium program made verification even more important and difficult. The more easily hidden components of a uranium program would require a more intrusive verification regime than the one that North Korea balked at in 2008.

A freeze would leave North Korea with its nuclear weapons, which already threaten South Korea and Japan. Such an agreement would trigger allied concerns about the U.S. extended deterrence guarantee, including the nuclear umbrella, to South Korea and Japan. Allied anxiety over U.S. reliability would increase advocacy within South Korea for an independent indigenous nuclear weapons program and greater reliance on preemption strategies.

Pyongyang may be willing to talk – but not about the topic of paramount U.S. concern: the denuclearization required by UN resolutions to which Pyongyang previously committed several times, but failed to fulfill.

Tightening the Economic Noose - Targeting North Korea's Cash Flow
Increased financial sanctions, combined with the increasing pariah status of the regime from its human rights violations, are leading nations to reduce the flow of hard currency to North Korea. While sanctions only apply to prohibited activities, even legitimate North Korean enterprises are becoming less profitable.

Numerous countries are severing their business relationships with North Korea by suspending economic deals, curtailing North Korean worker visas, and ejecting North Korean diplomats.
- **South Korea** terminated its involvement in the inter-Korean economic venture at Kaesong. South Korea's action severed a critical source of foreign currency for North Korea. Kaesong generated 23 percent of North Korea's foreign trade ($2.3 billion of North Korea's annual overall trade of $9.9 billion) and $120 million in annual profits.[1]

---

[1] Kim Tong-hyung, "How Impoverished but Nuclear-armed North Korea Earns Money," *The Morning Journal*, February 12, 2016, http://www.morningjournal.com/article/MJ/20160212/NEWS/160219852 and "S. Korea starts withdrawing nationals from Kaesong complex," Yonhap, February 11, 2016, http://english.yonhapnews.co.kr/northkorea/2016/02/11/64/0401000000AEN20160211002800315F.html.

17

- **Russian** state-run gas company Gazprom ended plans for energy-related projects with North Korea due to concerns arising from UN sanctions.[2]
- **Taiwan** implemented a complete ban on imports of North Korean coal, iron ore, and some other minerals.[3]
- **Uganda** directed that all North Korean military and police personnel should depart the country and that it was severing military and security ties with Pyongyang, which had been a source of revenue for the regime. There were approximately 50 North Korean military and police training officials. UN resolutions preclude North Korea from engaging in weapons trades or military training with other countries.[4]
- **Sudan** severed military ties with North Korea. In November 2016, Sudanese Foreign Minister Ibrahim Ghandour declared there were no longer any military or diplomatic cooperation with North Korea and that all diplomats had been removed.[5]
- **Namibia** halted economic ties with two North Korean state-run companies which had built a munitions factory, a violation of UN resolutions. The North Korean entities were Korea Mining Development Trading Corporation (KOMID), which is on the UN list of sanctioned entities for earning foreign cash via illicit arms deals, and its affiliate Mansudae Overseas Projects.[6] Africa has been an important arms market for North Korea.
- **Angola** suspended all commercial trade with North Korea,[7] **South Africa** stopped military cooperation and weapons deals,[8] and **Uzbekistan** demanded the departure of all North Korean diplomats and the closure of the North Korean embassy.[9]
- **Bangladesh, South Africa, Burma**, and other countries have expelled North Korean diplomats for illicit activities.[10]

North Korean Overseas Financial Operations Suffering

- **Conventional Arms Sales.** North Korea officials tied to illegal sales of conventional arms were deported from **Burma, Egypt, and Vietnam**. Pyongyang reportedly earned $300 million in hard currency from arms sales in 2015.[11] In March, **China** arrested dozens of smugglers involved in illegal arms trafficking with North Korea.
- **Overseas Restaurants.** Kim Jong-un expanded North Korean restaurants overseas to generate additional money for the regime. A high-ranking North Korean military defector estimated the regime's restaurants in **China** contributed $200 million annually to the

[2] "N.Korean Arms Dealers Run Out of Safe Havens." *The Chosun Ilbo*, April 29, 2016, http://english.chosun.com/site/data/html_dir/2016/04/29/2016042901075.html.
[3] Park Boram, "Tightening global sanctions hurting N. Korea's diplomatic ties, overseas commerce," Yonhap news, September 29, 2016.
[4] Kang Jin-kyu and Jeong Yong-soo, "Uganda tells North Koreans to go back home." *Korea Joongang Daily*, June 9, 2016, http://koreajoongangdaily.joins.com/news/article/Article.aspx?aid=3019773.
[5] Leo Byrne, "Sudan cuts military ties with North Korea," NK News, November 2, 2016.
[6] "Namibia cuts ties with North Korea state firms: South Korea government, media," Reuters, July 1, 2016, http://www.reuters.com/article/us-northkorea-namibia-idUSKCN0ZH3PW.
[7] "Squeezing North Korea: Old Friends Take Steps to Isolate Regime," Reuters. September 26, 2016.
[8] "12 Countries Downgrade Ties with N.Korea." Chosun Ilbo, October 4, 2016.
[9] Lee Yong-soo, "N.Korean Embassy in Uzbekistan Shut Down," Chosun Ilbo, August 22, 2016.
[10] Daniel Russel, "Statement Before the Senate Foreign Relations Committee, Subcommittee on East Asia, the Pacific, and International Cybersecurity Policy," September 28, 2016.
[11] "N.Korean Arms Dealers Run Out of Safe Havens," *The Chosun Ilbo*, April 29, 2016, http://english.chosun.com/site/data/html_dir/2016/04/29/2016042901075.html.

regime.[12] At least 30 of North Korea's overseas restaurants have closed due to dwindling business brought on by sanctions, China's anti-hedonism rules, and the South Korean government calling on its citizens to avoid the restaurants. [13]

- **Trading Companies.** North Korean trading companies in China to earn hard currency began defaulting on payments to Chinese creditors and began having difficulty acquiring lines of credit. A North Korean source reported, "Companies under the Ministry of External Economic Affairs and other trade agencies have [since April] begun experiencing a severe foreign currency crisis." Even Prime Minister Pak Pong-ju and Office 39, the North Korean leadership's money laundering organization, suffered foreign currency shortages.[14]

- **Transportation Organizations. Cambodia, Mongolia and Singapore** have revoked their permission for North Korean ships to sail under their national flag, which Pyongyang had used to evade sanctions.[15] North Korea's Ocean Maritime Management Company, sanctioned by the UN, has been essentially shut down and its ships denied access to ports.[16] **Kuwait, Thailand, and Pakistan** no longer allow Air Koryo to land in their countries, leaving only Russia and China as allowing flights.[17]

- **Overseas Workers. Malta, Poland, and Qatar** have stopped issuing work visas to North Korean workers in response to human rights abuses.[18] **Oman** repatriated 300 North Korean workers who had been involved in construction projects in response to greater international scrutiny.[19] **Singapore** will tighten control on North Korea immigrants by revoking North Korea's visa waiver status. Singapore was one of the few countries that allowed North Korean citizens to enter without a visa.[20] In March 2017, Malaysia cancelled its visa waiver program with North Korea after the assassination of Kim Jong-nam at the airport in Kuala Lumpur. The South Korean foreign ministry indicated that other countries in Africa, the

---

[12] Choi Song Min, "From cash cow to moribund in a matter of months," Daily NK. June 8, 2016, http://www.dailynk.com/english/read.php?catald=nk00300&num=13932.

[13] Choi Song Min, "From cash cow to moribund in a matter of months," June 8, 2016, Daily NK. http://www.dailynk.com/english/read.php?catald=nk00300&num=13932 and Jiang Jie, "NK restaurants in China falter as staff defect, profits decline," Global Times, May 25, 2016, http://www.dailynk.com/english/read.php?catald=nk00300&num=13932.

[14] Joshua Stanton, "North Korean trading companies can't pay their Chinese creditors because of sanctions," One Free Korea, June 22, 2016, http://freekorea.us/2016/06/22/north-korean-trading-companies-cant-pay-chinese-creditors-because-of-sanctions/ and Choi Song Min, "Sanctions drive trading companies to default on payments," Daily NK, June 21, 2016, http://www.dailynk.com/english/read.php?num=13953&catald=nk01500.

[15] Park Boram, "Tightening global sanctions hurting N. Korea's diplomatic ties, overseas commerce," Yonhap news, September 29, 2016 and [15] Daniel Russel, "Statement Before the Senate Foreign Relations Committee, Subcommittee on East Asia, the Pacific, and International Cybersecurity Policy," September 28, 2016.

[16] Daniel Russel, "Statement Before the Senate Foreign Relations Committee, Subcommittee on East Asia, the Pacific, and International Cybersecurity Policy," September 28, 2016.

[17] "N. Korea's Air Koryo operates flights to only China, Russia," Korea Times, October 25, 2016.

[18] Hyun Yun-kyung and Lee Joon-seung, "Malta has stopped issuing work visas for N.Koreas: foreign minister," Yonyap, July 31, 2016, http://english.yonhapnews.co.kr/northkorea/2016/07/31/0401000000AEN20160731000200315.html.

[19] http://www.upi.com/Top_News/World-News/2016/12/29/Hundreds-of-North-Korea-workers-in-Oman-sent-home-report-says/2551483031058/

[20] Countries that continue to provide visa waiver to North Korea are Dominican Republic, Ecuador, Haiti, Malaysia, Gambia, and few other small countries. "Singapore to exclude N.Korea from visa waiver countries list in October," Yonhap, July 31, 2016, http://english.yonhapnews.co.kr/news/2016/07/31/0200000000AEN20160731002100315.html?input=sns.

Middle East and Europe have also taken steps to reduce the number of North Korean laborers.[21]

Raising the Cost of North Korean Defiance

Each individual action to constrict North Korea's trade may not be decisive, but cumulatively these efforts reduce North Korea's foreign revenue sources, increase strains on the regime, and generate internal pressure. Collectively, the sanctions and measures to target North Korea's financial resources are forcing the regime to switch to less effective means to acquire and transfer currency as well as increasing stress on elites and the regime.

Sanctions and targeted financial measures serve a number of purposes:
- Enforce U.S. law and UN resolutions;
- Impose penalties on those that violate laws and sent a signal to other potential violators that prohibited nuclear programs comes with high economic and diplomatic costs;
- Raise the costs and slow the development of North Korea's development of nuclear and missile arsenals;
- Augment measures to constrain the import of items for North Korea's prohibited nuclear and missile programs;
- Strengthen non-proliferation measures;
- Disrupt North Korean illicit activities, including illegal drug manufacturing and trafficking, currency counterfeiting, money-laundering, and support to terrorist group;
- Highlight human rights abuses to drive nations away from conducting business with the heinous regime;
- Raise the risks for entities doing business with Pyongyang by eliminating their ability to access the U.S. financial network;
- Reduce North Korea's financial and trade linkages to the outside world and constrain the regime's money-making operations to induce more defections, closure of less profitable operations overseas, and a liquidity crisis;
- Use pressure from without to create greater internal pressure and fissures within the regime. Decreasing , induce more defections and acts of domestic resistance, and put regime stability at risk; and
- In conjunction with all the other instruments of national power, reshape North Korea's perception of the costs of violating UN resolutions and laws and persuade the regime to comply with UN resolutions and its previous denuclearization commitments.

Although North Korea has been subject to sanctions for decades, targeted financial measures (smart sanctions) have only been recently imposed on North Korea and half-heartedly at that due to Obama Administration timidity. It can well be argued that sanctions were not effectively imposed until 2016 with a stronger UN resolution and the Congressional-initiated North Korea Sanctions and Policy Enhancement Act. The latter was an attempt to induce the Obama Administration to more fully enforce US law.

---

[21] "Poland stops receiving N. Korean workers amid sanctions." Yonhap. June 7, 2016, http://english.yonhapnews.co.kr/northkorea/2016/06/07/0401000000AEN20160607009900315.html.

Follow (and Seize) The Money

North Korea adapted to increasing international pressure by altering its modus operandi, shifting networks, using shell companies, and fabricating documents. As Pyongyang shifted to Chinese brokers more integrated into the global economy, it *increased* North Korea's exposure and vulnerability to international pressure.

But U.S. law enforcement agencies didn't keep pace. Sanctions enforcement must be flexible, innovative, and adaptive to the changing tactics of the target, rather than abandoning efforts to uphold law and order as having become too difficult.

Washington should have begun including Chinese violators on the U.S. sanctions But the Obama Administration resisted doing so. A Stockholm International Peace Research Institute study from 2014 found that 91% of US and 84% of UN targeted entities were North Korean, but that 74% of sanctions evading networks identified in the report were third country (non-North Korea) entities.

Time to Break Some China

In September 2016, the Treasury and Justice Departments sanctioned five Chinese entities for laundering money using shell companies to surreptitiously moving funds through US banks. The Hongxiang Industrial Development Corporation had engaged in $532 million worth of trade with North Korea during 2011 to 2015. The action, required by the NKSPEA, was the first time the Obama Administration sanctioned a Chinese entity for providing assistance to North Korea's nuclear weapons program.

In March 2017, the U.S. imposed a $1.2 billion fine on Chinese telecommunication firm ZTE for violating export sanctions to Iran and North Korea. The U.S. actions could have a chilling effect on other Chinese banks and businesses engaging with North Korea.

While sanctions opponents assert that Beijing will not go along with U.S. sanctions, Washington can influence the behavior of Chinese banks and businesses that engage with North Korea through the use of targeted financial measures. When Washington took action against Macau-based Banco Delta Asia in 2005, labeling it a money-laundering concern, U.S. officials traveled throughout Asia, inducing 24 entities – including the Bank of China -- to cease economic engagement with North Korea.

U.S. officials indicate that the Bank of China defied the government of China in severing its ties with North Korea lest the bank face U.S. sanctions itself. The action showed that U.S. government actions can persuade Chinese financial entities to act in their self-interest even against the wished of the Chinese government.

The NKSPEA mandates secondary sanctions on third-country (including Chinese) banks and companies that violate U.N. sanctions and U.S. law. It forces them to choose between access to the U.S. economy and the North Korean economy. The U.S. should penalize entities, particularly Chinese financial institutions and businesses, that trade with those on the sanctions list or export prohibited items. The U.S. should also ban financial institutions that conduct business with North Korean violators from access to the U.S. financial network.

Put North Korea Back on the Terrorist List

The Bush Administration removed Pyongyang from the State Sponsors of Terrorism list in 2008 in a failed attempt to stimulate progress in the Six-Party Talks nuclear negotiations. Since its removal from the terrorism list, Pyongyang has conducted several terrorist acts, including deadly attacks against North Korean defectors abroad:

- In 2014, North Korea conducted a cyber attack against Sony pictures for producing a film critical of North Korean leader Kim Jong-un. Pyongyang also threatened "9/11-type attacks" against U.S. theaters showing the film.
- In 2009, 2011, 2012, and 2013, Seoul concluded that North Korea was behind cyber attacks using viruses or distributed denial-of-service tactics against South Korean government agencies, businesses, banks, and media organizations.
- In June 2012, Seoul Metropolitan Police arrested a South Korean man for violating the National Security Law. The man had met in China with agents of the North Korean ruling party's General Reconnaissance Bureau to purchase software with malignant viruses that were used to conduct a cyber-attack on Incheon International Airport.
- In May 2012, North Korea jammed GPS signals affecting hundreds of civilian airliners flying in and out of South Korea. The Korea Communications Commission stated that the signals came from North Korea.
- In April 2012, North Korean agent An Hak-young was sentenced to four years imprisonment by a South Korean court for plotting to assassinate outspoken anti-Pyongyang activist Park Sang-hak with a poison-tipped needle.
- In July 2010, two agents of the North Korean General Reconnaissance Bureau were arrested and pled guilty before a South Korean court to attempting to assassinate high-level defector Hwang Jang-Yop, who was residing in South Korea. Kim Myung-ho and Do Myung-kwan were sentenced to 10 years in jail.
- In December 2009, Thai authorities seized 35 tons of North Korean weapons, including rockets and rocket-propelled grenades that were determined to be en route to terrorist groups Hamas and Hezbollah.
- In 2009, three shipments of North Korean conventional arms bound for Iran were seized. Western and Israeli intelligence officials believe the shipments were bound for Hamas and Hezbollah. Kim admitted to being an agent of the North Korean General Reconnaissance Bureau and having been ordered to assassinate Hwang.
- In October 2008, a North Korean woman was convicted by a South Korean court for plotting to kill South Korean intelligence agents with poisoned needles.

As one component of a broader U.S. strategy toward North Korea, the Trump Administration should return Pyongyang to the State Sponsors of Terrorism List. Under 18 U.S. Code § 2331, international terrorism is defined as acts that:

> (A) involve violent acts or acts dangerous to human life that are a violation of the criminal laws of the United States or of any State, or that would be a criminal violation if committed within the jurisdiction of the United States or of any State;
> (B) appear to be intended—
>> (i) to intimidate or coerce a civilian population;
>> (ii) to influence the policy of a government by intimidation or coercion; or
>> (iii) to affect the conduct of a government by mass destruction, assassination, or kidnapping; and

(C) occur primarily outside the territorial jurisdiction of the United States, or transcend national boundaries in terms of the means by which they are accomplished, the persons they appear intended to intimidate or coerce, or the locale in which their perpetrators operate or seek asylum.

Returning North Korea to the terrorist list would be a proper and pragmatic recognition of regime behavior that violated U.S. statutes. It would also have tangible impact on regime finances. It would enable invoking stronger financial transaction licensing requirements under 31 CFR Part 596 vs. 31 CFR Part 510 and remove North Korea's sovereign immunity from civil liability for terrorist acts. Redesignation would require the U.S. government to oppose loans to North Korea by international financial institutions, such as the World Bank, International Monetary Fund, and Asian Development Bank.

The designation would also assist the international effort to increase North Korea's diplomatic and economic isolation for its actions. Last year, several countries and companies severed their business relationships due to North Korea's violations, the abysmal conditions its overseas laborers worked under, and its human rights violations deemed by the UN to constitute "crimes against humanity." Designating North Korea as a state sponsor of terrorism could induce additional business partners to avoiding dealing with such a heinous regime.

Impose Sanctions for Human Rights Abuses
In July 2016, the Obama administration imposed sanctions on North Korean leader Kim Jong-un, 10 other individuals, and five entities "for their ties to North Korea's notorious abuses of human rights." It was the first time that the U.S. had designated North Korean entities for human rights abuses.

The action cut the entities off from the U.S. financial system and made it more risky for any institution to hold or move the money on behalf of North Korea. It also "has a worldwide ripple effect. Banks and financial institutions outside the U.S. use OFAC's SDN list and follow it as a measure of risk [and] compliance."[22]

Sanctioning Kim Jong-un and others will not only have a direct financial impact on the North Korean regime, but could also have powerful secondary reverberations for the pariah regime. Concern over potential secondary liability, or of keeping company with perpetrators of crimes against humanity, could galvanize other nations to reduce or sever their economic interaction with such a heinous regime.

The U.S. should expand the list of human rights violating entities subject to sanctions.

Improve Information Access in North Korea[23]
Promoting democracy and access to information in North Korea is in both the strategic and humanitarian interests of the United States. But getting information into North Korea is no

---

[22] "Background Briefing on DPRK the Human Rights Abuser Report and Sanctions," Special Briefing with Senior Administration Officials, July 6, 2016.
[23] I am indebted to my Heritage Foundation colleague Olivia Enos for her advocacy on augmenting information access for this section of my testimony.

23

easy feat. The regimes information blockade ranges from instituting an internal internet server, to limitations on the number of accessible radio stations, to prohibitions on the type of books that can be read. Persons caught with a Bible, for example, or unapproved Western literature, often face consequences as severe as death.[24]

International efforts to penetrate the information firewall in North Korea have thus far focused primarily on radios, DVDs, and cell phones. However, new technology is offering more innovative ways to get information into North Korea which the U.S. should incorporate into its strategy to promote information access in North Korea.

There are three main ways to access outside information in North Korea: radio; electronic devices like USB drives, DVDs, CDs; and cell phones. Emerging technology presents opportunities to disseminate information in new ways that may improve information access in the DPRK.

To find new methods of cross-border data penetration, Silicon Valley entrepreneurs and programmers gathered at Hack North Korea, an event organized by the Human Rights Foundation (HRF).[25] Some new ideas discussed at the event included the use of compact satellite dishes which are easily concealed and have the potential to receive signals from South Korean broadcasts, and smart balloons with a propeller and GPS unit for dropping leaflets, DVDs, and USBs more effectively. The HRF is looking for other ways to advance technologies that disrupt the DPRK's information monopoly.

The following additional steps should be taken to help increase North Koreans' access to outside information:

- Use grants appropriated under the 2004 North Korea Human Rights Act to invest in new technologies that improve information access in North Korea. Ideas generated at Google and the HRF should be further explored and once developed, applied.
- The U.S. government should encourage the South Korean government to grant NGOs access to AM frequencies. South Korea should take the approach that the more information that gets into North Korea, the better. As such, Seoul should go beyond merely funding government broadcasts. At the very least, the government should not obstruct commendable NGO efforts to improve information access in the DPRK.
- The U.S. and South Korea should evaluate radio messaging to ensure it is relevant to North Korean audiences. Interviews with defectors reveal that (1) North Koreans have limited access to NGO broadcasts, but upon leaving North Korea they realized that NGO broadcasting was more relevant than government-run broadcasts; and (2) North Koreans prefer entertainment-oriented broadcasts to the analytical and often demeaning news broadcasts disseminated through government programming.

[24] Fox News, "North Korea Publicly Executes 80, Some for Videos or Bibles, Report Says," November 12, 2013, http://www.foxnews.com/world/2013/11/12/north-korea-publicly-executes-80-for-crimes-like-watching-films-owning-bible.html.
[25] Human Rights Foundation, "Hack North Korea," https://humanrightsfoundation.org/programs/hrf-programs/hack-north-korea.

24

Conclusion

Washington must sharpen the choice for North Korea by raising the risk and cost for its actions as well as for those, particularly Beijing, who have been willing to facilitate the regime's prohibited programs and illicit activities and condone its human rights violations.

Sanctions require time and the political will to maintain them in order to work. While there are additional measures that can and should be applied, more important is to vigorously and assiduously implement existing UN measures and U.S. laws. We must approach sanctions, pressure, and isolation in a sustained and comprehensive way. It is a policy of a slow python constriction rather than a rapid cobra strike.

North Korea must feel unbearable pain from sanctions to the point that it sees regime existence is under threat. Pyongyang shouldn't feel a pinch from sanctions but rather a swift kick to the groin. The reality is that we are seeking to create conditions for bringing about a change in the regime while engaging in a long-term containment policy.

25

* * * * * * * * * * * * * * * * * *

The Heritage Foundation is a public policy, research, and educational organization recognized as exempt under section 501(c)(3) of the Internal Revenue Code. It is privately supported and receives no funds from any government at any level, nor does it perform any government or other contract work.

The Heritage Foundation is the most broadly supported think tank in the United States. During 2016, it had hundreds of thousands of individual, foundation, and corporate supporters representing every state in the U.S. Its 2016 income came from the following sources:

Individuals 75.3%

Foundations 20.3%

Corporations 1.8%

Program revenue and other income 2.6%

The top five corporate givers provided The Heritage Foundation with 1.0% of its 2016 income. The Heritage Foundation's books are audited annually by the national accounting firm of RSM US, LLP.

Mr. YOHO. Mr. Klingner, I appreciate it.

Dr. Lee, if you would, please.

STATEMENT OF SUNG-YOON LEE, PH.D., KIM KOO-KOREA FOUNDATION PROFESSOR IN KOREAN STUDIES AND ASSISTANT PROFESSOR, THE FLETCHER SCHOOL OF LAW AND DIPLOMACY, TUFTS UNIVERSITY

Mr. LEE. Thank you, Mr. Chairman, distinguished members of the subcommittee.

With your permission, I would like to make five points in the following order: First, I would like to mention the mundane, and then proceed to comment on the arcane, the inane, the profane, and the humane.

First the mundane. North Korea is a Korean state vying for legitimacy against a far more successful, attractive Korean state. The basic internal dynamic in the Korean Peninsula almost dictates that North Korea try to maximize its one strategic advantage over its neighbor. By the conventional industries of measuring state power, military power, political economic power, territorial size, soft power, North Korea does not fare very well against its southern neighbor except in the field of—except for military power. Therefore, the proposition that through artful diplomacy or a little bit of coercion, we can get North Korea to give up its nuclear weapons, as we did vis-a-vis the former Soviet republics of Kazakhstan, Belarus, Ukraine that inherited Soviet nukes, or South Africa, this is a tall order. It is quite unrealistic, in my opinion. So it is something new—a new approach is imperative at this point.

The arcane. I think in the wake of North Korea's third nuclear test in February 2013, the new, young Xi Jinping regime was quite irate, and they said a lot of things that seemed to please American ears in the spring of 2013: "We are going to put some hurt on them. We have finally come around. We are going to punish North Korea." This is pure illusion. Historically, North Korea has insulted, defied the top Chinese leaders far more egregiously than in 2013. Always, the Chinese grit their teeth, increase aid. And, indeed, in 2013, China-North Korea trade increased to $6.5 billion, an all-time high.

May I just give you one example, historical example. In 1982, September, Kim Il Sung visited China, met with Deng Xiaoping and the top leaders, pleaded with the Chinese leadership to approve the hereditary succession of power from father to son, which is a sensitive topic in the communist system, it is a contradiction. Then the next summer, Kim Jong Il made a trip personally and met with Deng Xiaoping and used Deng Xiaoping as a foil, as a smokescreen for his plan to lay a bomb for the visiting South Korean President in Burma in October 1983.

China, listening to North Korea's request, conveyed to the Reagan administration repeatedly the message that, you can do business with these people, you can talk to them, please. Deng Xiaoping told the visiting Secretary of Defense, Caspar Weinberger, on September 28 that message. That very same day, Deng Xiaoping also agreed to give North Korea 20 former Soviet MiG-21-type fighter jets.

Now, when the bomb went off on October 9, Deng Xiaoping lost face. He was very irate. He said Kim Jong Il will never, as long as I live, be able to set his foot on Chinese soil, and he didn't until 2000, the year 2000. Yet, Deng Xiaoping honored the agreement to provide North Korea with warplanes.

My point here is China has a strategic interest in the Korean Peninsula that defies moral principles, that defies security interests of the United States.

The profane. I don't mean North Korea's propensity to hurl insults at American and South Korean leaders. What I refer to is North Korea's state policy of using food as a weapon, North Korea's policy of mass, deliberate mass starvation, as the U.N. Commission of Inquiry of 2014 alleges. This is a very serious allegation. The U.N. Commission of Inquiry Report on Human Rights in North Korea states that North Korea's crimes against humanity have "no parallel in the contemporary world." The section on the violation of the right to food and other related aspects of the right to life, pages 144 to 208, merits close reading.

This is the kind of regime that we are dealing with, a regime that enjoys a tremendous advantage of industrialization, urbanization, nearly 100 percent literacy among the population; yet, is among the top nations of the world every year, every single year, afflicted with serious food insecurity. This is the product of the determined, perverse policy of the state, not U.S. sanctions or climate change or poor soil, poor weather, and so forth.

Lastly, the humane. I think human rights is essential to our policy toward North Korea, because, as I mentioned, starvation, hunger, these are visceral, universal human emotions that can be understood quite easily. It will be very helpful in pushing for more human rights operations, information dissemination into North Korea so that the world, that the world public opinion changes in our favor, and that we name and shame North Korea, and that we educate the North Korean people of the true nature of the regime and try to invite them to take the risk of crossing the border into a free Korean state.

Thank you.

[The prepared statement of Mr. Lee follows:]

Testimony of Sung-Yoon Lee
Kim Koo-Korea Foundation Professor in Korean Studies and Assistant Professor
The Fletcher School of Law and Diplomacy, Tufts University

Subcommittee on Asia and the Pacific, Foreign Affairs Committee,
U.S. House of Representatives
"Pressuring North Korea: Evaluating Options"
March 21, 2017

Thank you, Mr. Chairman, and distinguished members of the Subcommittee:

I am honored to have this opportunity to present my views on how best to stem North Korea's
growing threat from its illicit ballistic missile and nuclear programs.

I. Rethink North Korea Policy

i. North Korea's "Exceptionable Exceptionalism"

First, the world must dispossess itself of the notion that North Korea may be charmed out of its
ballistic missile and nuclear path through conventional diplomacy of quid pro quo boosted by
moral suasion. Of the world's nine nuclear states, North Korea arguably is more resistant to
denuclearization than the U.K. or France—states that face neither questions of legitimacy from
an alternate British or French state nor a direct threat from its neighbor—and just as resistant to
denuclearization as India, Pakistan, and Israel. Over the past quarter century, the Kim regime's
cultish "mockability"[1] and the bedeviled nation's acute poverty have fed the fancy that for the
right price Pyongyang may be persuaded to dismantle its WMD programs.

However, the reality has been and, shall remain, that as long as Pyongyang is not presented with
the risk of regime instability, it will not only grasp onto its WMDs but continue to bolster them
at a crushing cost to its own people. The internal dynamic of the Korean peninsula, in which two
states vie for pan-Korean legitimacy, dictates that the despotic, illegitimate, and eminently risible
regime do all it can to extort the democratic, legitimate, attractive other. For the Kim regime,
nuclear-armed missiles are not a "bargaining chip" or "deterrent." They are the one panacea that
may one day overturn all gloomy indices of state inferiority vis-à-vis the Republic of Korea. In
other words, they are both the very means to the regime's long-term survival and its end game of
prevailing over the South.

Short of sustained pressure by the U.S. and its allies that presents Pyongyang with pressing
existential questions that compel it to rethink its state priorities, the North Korea threat will only
continue to grow bigger. This is a risk that the U.S. must bear. It is clear now that the era of
passivity, procrastination, and half-measures has come to its close, and the United States and its

---

[1] It may not be a proper word. The author is unable to find it in any dictionary. At the same time, the intended
connotation, if not meaning, here is apparent.

allies have entered a period of consequences. How the Trump administration meets North Korea's growing lethal threat will have grave implications on regional peace, global proliferation security, human security, and the credibility of the U.S. as a great power.

ii. Dispel Despair

Second, the world must dispossess itself, when it comes to North Korea, of the temptation to be resigned to the notion that "there are no good options" or that "sanctions don't work." Rare is the garland of attractive options when it comes to nuclear politics, which, short of waging war, is international politics at the highest level. And sanctions take time and uniform enforcement to bear fruit. North Korea's systemic vulnerabilities actively invite exploitation by the U.S. and its allies. What has been lacking is the political will and sufficient government support in both human financial resources to enable the exploitation of such systemic weaknesses.

The North Korean regime's continuing dependence on illicit international financial transactions in U.S. dollars as an instrument of regime preservation begs exploitation by the United States. Recent annual reports by the UN Panel of Experts on North Korea all note that in spite of North Korea's multifaceted tactics of circumventing UN Security Council-mandated sanctions and inadequate enforcement or non-compliance by member states, Pyongyang's choice of currency for international transactions still remains the U.S. dollar.[2] Moreover, for sanctions to take their intended full effect, they must be applied and uniformly enforced by various parties over several years. Sanctions must be enforced free of political expedients—the impulse to relax them or provide Pyongyang with negating subsidies in the face of its next escalation. This principle applies to all parties, including the U.S., South Korea, and Japan alike. Furthermore, the Kim regime's illegitimacy and seven decades-long record of crimes against humanity leave it open to erosion-from-within. That the totalitarian regime thus far has been successful in repressing its own people and blocking the flow of information in and out of its domain does not necessarily mean that this perverse equation cannot one day be overturned. The U.S. and its regional allies have much to gain in vastly increasing funding for information and broadcasting dissemination efforts into the closed, information-deprived country.

---

[2] The 2015 UN Panel of Experts report states, "In most cases investigated by the Panel, transactions were made in United States dollars from foreign-based banks and transferred through corresponding bank accounts in the United States." S/2015/131, Paragraph 190 (69). http://www.un.org/ga/search/view_doc.asp?symbol=S/2015/131
The 2016 report also states, "Transactions originating in foreign banks have been processed through corresponding banks in the United States and Europe." S/2016/157. Paragraph 180 (62).
http://www.un.org/ga/search/view_doc.asp?symbol=S/2016/157
The 2017 report also states that North Korea "continues to access the international financial system to support its activities." S/2017/150. Paragraph 210 (71). http://www.un.org/ga/search/view_doc.asp?symbol=S/2017/150

iii. Co-opt China

Third, China's strategic interests in the Korean peninsula will shift toward pressuring the Kim Jong Un regime to the point of destabilizing it *only* when China itself is confronted with a serious and imminent security, economic, or humanitarian threat. Engineering a security or humanitarian crisis for China is hardly a feasible option, whereas raising the financial cost of coddling Pyongyang for China is firmly within the U.S. diplomatic arsenal and legal authority. China today enjoys greater political and economic influence over the Korean peninsula than at any time since its defeat in the First Sino-Japanese War of 1894-1895, which largely removed China from Korean affairs until the founding of the People's Republic in 1949 and forestalled official relations with South Korea until the normalization of relations in 1992. A nuclear Pyongyang that steadfastly showers Beijing with the gift of the "North Korea card" to be played against Washington in China's long-term strategic competition against the U.S. is arguably of greater utility to China than a North Korea denuclearized. Moreover, South Korea's total volume of trade with China significantly exceeds that with the U.S. and Japan put together, with Seoul enjoying each year tens of billions of dollars in trade surplus over Beijing.[3] Thus, both Koreas remain in varying degrees beholden to China, which means China will see no compelling reason to put real pressure on Pyongyang unless the status quo becomes a high risk for itself. American exhortations of China's need to be a "responsible stakeholder" (2006) and frequent pleas for help since notwithstanding, China will only change when the carrying cost of coddling the Kim regime grows from costly to costlier—or critical.

Under the current dynamics in the region, China will remain more an obstacle than key to North Korea's denuclearization. The road to North Korea's denuclearization indeed lies through China, but only through a China incentivized by economic disincentives to change course and, out of pragmatic considerations, apply, even if begrudgingly, increasing pressure on Pyongyang's international finances.

II. Three Common Myths

i. Pyongyang Listens to Beijing

Since the advent of the Xi Jinping era in late 2012, the Kim Jong Un regime has conducted three nuclear tests and three long-range missile tests.[4] Each incident has meant some loss of face for

---

[3] Korea Customs Service statistics for 2016 indicate that South Korea reaped approximately $37 billion trade surplus vis-à-vis China, while Seoul's surplus in total trade with the U.S. and Japan were approximately $2 billion. Korea Customs Service," Import/Export by Country," 2016 and 2017. http://english.customs.go.kr/kcshome/trade/TradeCountryList.do?layoutMenuNo=21031

[4] The three nuclear tests were carried out on the following dates: February 12, 2013, during the Chinese New Year Holiday; January 6, 2016, two days before Kim Jong Un's birthday; and September 9, 2016, On National Founding Day. The three long-range missile tests were conducted on: April 13, 2012, two days shy of Kim Il Sung's centennial celebrations; December 12, 2012, just one week before South Korea's presidential election; and February 7, 2016, just one month after the regime's fourth nuclear test.

China. Xi and Kim have yet to meet in person, and, in recent weeks, China has taken a sterner approach to North Korea, such as the ban on coal import from North Korea for the remainder of 2017. Such signs of rift in the bilateral relationship suggest to some that Beijing is quite displeased with Pyongyang and may be amenable to punishing it in ways worthy of the name. Some commentators have even remarked that Sino-North Korean relations are now at an all-time low. But, in fact, the less-than-cozy relationship over the past several years is more a typical transitory phase rather than an aberration. It is certainly not a nadir in the bilateral relationship. For example, relations in the mid-1960s were marked by a border skirmish, recalling of respective ambassadors, colorful name-calling at each other, and Pyongyang's tilt to Moscow. But, after about four years, the relationship was renewed with generous aid from Beijing. Historically, when Sino-North Korean relations are visibly discourteous or even acrimonious, Beijing, after a decent interval, is more prone to reward Pyongyang with new and greater economic/military concessions rather than punish it.

Hence, short of North Korean behavior or developments inside the North flaring into an imminent security threat to China itself, Beijing is hardly likely to penalize Pyongyang in any real sense even as it signs on to UN Security Council resolutions calling for more punitive economic measures. While it may seem counterintuitive, the record over the past 60 years suggests that the more North Korea irritates China, the more aid and political support Beijing gives Pyongyang out of strategic interests in the region. This argument, even if partially valid, should give pause to the U.S. and its allies as they once again look to China to exercise its vast economic and political influence on Pyongyang in the wake of its ongoing provocations.

In August 1956, Kim Il Sung, the founder and grandfather of the current North Korean leader, began a campaign of bloody purges against pro-Chinese and pro-Soviet factions in the party. The response by Kim's patron states was a dispatch of a high-level joint punitive expedition to Pyongyang in September. Anastas Mikoyan, a high-ranking member of the Politburo, while attending a Chinese Communist Party congress in Beijing in September, coordinated with General Peng Dehuai, the Chinese commander in the Korean War, and together with their deputies flew into Pyongyang to admonish the North Korean leader.[5] The joint foreign delegation demanded that Kim restore expelled opposition leaders to their former positions. The North Korean leader, taken aback and humiliated, consented to cease all purges. However, within a year of the Sino-Soviet intervention, Kim resumed his attack on his opponents that resulted in thousands of dismissals from the Korean Workers' Party and tens of thousands imprisoned and executed. In effect, Kim Il Sung had set the tone for his regime's future relations with Beijing and Moscow. Mao Zedong even apologized to Kim when the two met in Moscow in November 1957 for the first time since the dispatch of the high-level envoys to Pyongyang. Thereafter, not only would there be no heavy-handed approach from either Beijing or Moscow again, but with each apparent insult or provocative behavior by the North Korean leadership, for example, the seizure of the U.S.S Pueblo in January 1968 and the shootdown of the U.S. reconnaissance plane in April 1969, both patron states renewed and increased aid to Pyongyang.

---

[5] Shen Zhihua, "Alliance of 'Tooth and Lips' or Marriage of Convenience? The Origins of development of the Sino-North Korean Alliance, 1946-1958" (Washington, D.C.: U.S.-Korea Institute at SAIS, Working Paper Series, WP-09. December 2008).

China's leverage over North Korea in the late-1950s, in particular, with hundreds of thousands of Chinese troops still stationed in the North, was arguably greater than China's leverage over Pyongyang at any point in the post-Cold War period. Yet, China exercised self-restraint in the face of Pyongyang's defiance and in fact provided North Korea with the following concessions in 1958 alone: a long-term credit of $25 million, construction of a hydroelectric power station on the Yalu River, and an agreement on scientific and technical cooperation.[6] China also agreed to aid North Korea develop its shipbuilding, cement, fishing, and silk industries, while accepting North Korean students to receive technical training in China. For Kim Il Sung, the lessons must have been clear: It pays to stand up to the bigger powers as long as Kim remains within bounds, that is, as long as he is able to read the strategic environment and does not deviate too far from the socialist line of anti-imperialist revolutionary struggle—which, in modern parlance, would translate as "strategic provocations against the U.S."

Over the past decade, the record shows that China has increased trade with North Korea with each nuclear test by Pyongyang, even as it endorsed tougher UN Security Resolutions. This trend, short of a clear and present economic cost for Beijing, is expected to continue.

ii. Sanctions Don't Work

My esteemed colleagues, Joshua Stanton, Bruce Klingner, and Anthony Ruggiero, have done much to dispel the myth that U.S. sanctions against North Korea have reached their full capacity; that is, with respect to North Korea, U.S. sanctions have been exhausted. In fact, in both degree and kind, U.S. sanctions against North Korea have been relatively weak until just one year ago. The self-restraint exercised by the U.S. in implementing sanctions against Pyongyang has been reminiscent of the self-restraint shown in the wake of each lethal attack by North Korea against South Koreans and Americans in South Korea since the 1960s. Even in egregious cases of attack by North Korea that may be regarded as acts of war, there has there never been a military response by the U.S. No doubt, the risk of escalation and possible war in the Korean peninsula has impelled both the U.S. and South Korea to act with caution. Academically speaking, this may be viewed as the correct response—a prudent non-response that may have thwarted rapid escalation and perhaps even war. At the same time, it is undeniable that such reticence to respond with credible resolve or military force has conditioned Pyongyang to assume that it can get away with murder.

In recent years, overall U.S. policy toward North Korea has been tepid at best. Even nations that pose no security threat to the U.S., such as Belarus, Ukraine, Zimbabwe, and Burma have been more heavily sanctioned by the U.S. than North Korea, which, by all accounts, is among the world's leaders in arms proliferation and human rights violations. The only possible conclusion to be drawn from this kind of extraordinary self-restraint is that previous administrations have been self-deterred by concerns that in the event the U.S. aggressively blocks Pyongyang's

---

[6] *Peking Review*, 1:35, October 28, 1958.

streams of revenue and designates Chinese entities, North Korea may lash out (and even start a war) and China may start a trade war with the U.S.

However, the evidence is to the contrary. In the aftermath of the Treasury Department's designation of Banco Delta Asia a Primary Money Laundering Concern in September 2005, North Korea found itself isolated from the international financial order, even shunned by Chinese banks. The blow to Pyongyang was not that North Korean deposits of approximately $25 million in the bank were frozen, but that Treasury's blacklisting had deterred North Korea's partners from continuing to conduct business with Pyongyang as usual. While a plausible argument could be made that the Treasury's designation pushed Pyongyang to accelerate its first nuclear test, which took place on October 9, 2006, on the eve of Party Founding Day, it is certain that North Korea at some point thereafter would have crossed the nuclear Rubicon at a time of its choosing, spurred by both political and technological imperatives. Subsequent nuclear and missile tests have also been timed to maximize their impact. They have taken place on North Korean, American, and Chinese national holidays and on weekends—presumably to capture the global headlines and pressure Pyongyang's adversaries to come up with a response, which have been more often than not a return, following an interval marked by little more than rhetorical condemnations, to talks with even greater concessions in tow.

Furthermore, in May 2013, two months after Treasury designated North Korea's Foreign Trade Bank in the wake of Pyongyang's nuclear test in February, describing it as a "key financial node in North Korea's WMD apparatus" that "facilitate[s] transactions on behalf of actors linked to its proliferation networks," four of China's biggest banks—Industrial and Commercial Bank of China, Agricultural Bank of China, China Construction Bank, and Bank of China—all ceased money transfer with the North's Foreign Trade Bank. [7] Soon, the Foreign Trade Bank was blocked from the global financial system. However, because Pyongyang uses food insecurity as a weapon with which to make the people dependent on the regime for goods and extract aid from abroad, Pyongyang insisted that the NGOs operating inside North Korea continue to use only the Foreign Trade bank. As a result, aid workers lost their access to international banking services and ended up carrying bulk cash in bags from Beijing to Pyongyang. Some European aid workers decried the loss of access to the Foreign Trade Bank and, instead of using their considerable moral and material leverage to demand Pyongyang to abide by at least some semblance of international norms of transparency, chose to blame the U.S. rather than North Korea for the inconvenience.

Sustained financial sanctions against North Korean entities and their Chinese partners may raise tension with both nations in the short terms. At the same time, North Korea has shown itself not to be suicidal or "crazy," and has abided by a strategy of calculated provocations—lethal, at times, but always controlled and small-scale—at a time of its own choosing. In other words, Pyongyang's nuclear and missile tests are likely to proceed as planned almost *irrespective* of U.S. sanctions *or* negotiations. To posit that further sanctions may forestall denuclearization or lead to war is to deny the past several decades of history: Conventional diplomacy will only allow North Korea to buy time and the resources with which to advance its WMDs programs. On the other

---

[7] Joshua Stanton, "North Korea: The Myth of Maxed-Out Sanctions." *Fletcher Security Review*, January 21, 2015. http://www.fletchersecurity.org/stanton

hand, inflicting financial costs on North Korean and Chinese entities will have few, if any, deleterious effects on U.S. interests.

Moreover, the effectiveness of sanctions should not be evaluated solely on the criterion of transforming the target country's leadership but by the degree of gain in the sanctioning country's negotiating position relative to the sanctioned nation. By implementing these sanctions, is the U.S. likely to be in a stronger position to achieve a better eventual settlement with North Korea? In weighing U.S. interests vis-à-vis North Korea's, deterrence as well as denuclearization becomes a critical consideration. Thus, the utility of financial sanctions as a credible deterrent to Pyongyang's further nuclear and missile development and proliferation, at least in the short term, is a necessary condition to achieving the ultimate goal of denuclearization. In sum, these financial regulatory measures are the best way to present the Kim regime with a non-lethal-but-existential threat. On principle, too, they are the right thing to do. Such credible threats also have the best chance of achieving secondary or even tertiary objectives goals in any sanctions regime: protecting the integrity of the international system and symbolically enhancing the prestige of the sanctioning nation by making a moral statement. These measures also have the advantage of having the best chance of modifying the Kim regime's brutal treatment of its own people, even if change proves incremental and sporadic.

iii. Human Rights are Secondary Considerations

Among the grave findings by the landmark report by the UN Commission of Inquiry on Human Rights in North Korea, published in February 2014, is that the North Korean regime is guilty of virtually every single act of crimes against humanity as defined by the International Criminal Court, *as well as* the following, which is a novelty in international criminal law: The "inhumane act of knowing causing prolonged starvation."[8] North Korea's elites enjoy a life of extravagance while the vast majority of the people languish in miserable conditions under a brutal police state. This reality is the direct product of the Kim dynasty's determined policies over the past several decades, not the result of U.S. sanctions or unfavorable weather conditions, as some wish to believe. The Kim dynasty has assiduously misallocated its national resources and earnings from illicit financial transactions to its nuclear weapons and long-range ballistic missile programs, while allowing a very high percentage of its population to be hungry (above 80%), a substantial percentage of its people to be undernourished (42%), and untold many to waste away and starve to death.[9] In various UN reports, each year North Korea is rated among the world's three or four "top" nations by the matrix of undernourishment among the population, alternating between third and fourth place together with Zambia and the Central African Republic. Tellingly, North Korea stands alone among UN's list of nations most afflicted with chronic food insecurity: It is the only nation that is industrialized, urbanized, and literate. All others are impoverished, pre-industrial

---

[8] UN Office of the High Commissioner for Human Rights. "UN Commission of Inquiry on Human Rights in the Democratic People's Republic of Korea," February 17, 2014. http://www.ohchr.org/EN/NewsEvents/Pages/DisplayNews.aspx?NewsID=14255&LangID=E

[9] Food and Agriculture Organization of the UN. "The State of Food Insecurity in the World, 2015." 45-47. http://www.fao.org/3/a-i4646e.pdf

agrarian economies often beset by internal turmoil, in which illiteracy rates among the adult—especially the female—population range from the 20 to 70 percent.

North Korean people today need to be informed that their loved ones died during the famine in the mid- to late-1990s not because the regime was poor and did not have the funds with which to import food from abroad, but because of its perverse priorities. As tens hundreds of thousands died, the Kim Jong Un regime spent billions of dollars on defense and arms purchases, building the world's most extravagant mausoleum for Kim's deceased leader, preventing people from crossing into China in search of food, and proscribing food delivery to the Northeast region. Washington and, in particular, Seoul, should highlight the acute North Korean humanitarian crisis by drawing world public attention to the issue and increasing support of radio broadcasts and other information transmission efforts into North Korea. The Republic of Korea, as the sole legitimate representative government in the Korean peninsula, should take the leading role in this global human rights campaign. South Korea, the U.S., and Japan are also mandated by their own North Korean human rights acts to improve human rights in North Korea. They could and should cooperate closely together and sponsor—if necessary, through third civilian parties—reports, publications, international conventions, transmissions and dissemination of information related to North Korea's multifarious nefarious human-rights abuses throughout their respective countries and the world. The more people in democratic societies think about the North Korean regime as a threat to humanity and less as an idiosyncratic abstraction, the more they will be resolved not to allow their leaders to resort to politically expedient measures with each future provocation by Pyongyang or defer Korean reunification.

Nearly 50% of North Koreans who have defected to the South since the famine years say that they had come into contact with outside information primarily through South Korean TV shows on DVD and radio broadcasts, which served as an incentive to escape their nation. According to one survey, among North Korean defectors who have resettled in the South since 2009, 75 percent say they have been exposed to foreign media, with 25 percent reporting they had experienced heavy exposure.[10] Citizens in free societies would do well to remember that sending information into North Korea is not merely a defense of the principle of the freedom of information; rather, it is an act that saves real lives. In this effort, the U.S. can provide South Korea, Japan, and other free nations with moral, financial, technical, and logistical support.

An increase in budget for Korean language programs on Voice of America (VOA), Radio Free Asia (RFA), and broadcasters from other nations would enable greater broadcasting time, stronger signals, proliferation of self-tuning short-wave radios, greater variety of programs, expansion of the listening audience, and the much-needed education of the North Korean people, who are clearly the most cut-off people in the world. Section 301 of the North Korea Sanctions and Policy Enhancement Act of 2016 calls on the President to submit to Congress a "detailed plan for making unrestricted, unmonitored, and inexpensive electronic mass communications available to the people of North Korea." Both the legal mandate and moral imperative are present

[10] Nat Kretchun and Jane Kim, "A Quiet Opening: North Koreans in a Changing Media Environment," InterMedia, (2011). 84.
http://www.intermedia.org/wp-content/uploads/2013/05/A_Quiet_Opening_FINAL_InterMedia.pdf

for Congress to seize the initiative and overhaul U.S. information programs targeting North Korea.

The Broadcasting Board of Governors budget request for fiscal year 2017 shows that congressional funding for Korean services in recent years has been less than those for many other countries—both big and small. For example, in the case of VOA, funds requested for Korean services in 2017 are $2.9 million, whereas those requested for Burmese, Tibetan, Indonesian, and Mandarin Chinese services are, respectively, $3.1 million, $3.3 million, $6.1 million, and $12 million. Funds requested for RFA Korean services for 2017 are $2.4 million, while those for Tibetan and Mandarin Chinese services are, respectively, $4.1 million and $4.8 million.[11] Congress could authorize a substantial increase in funding for Korean services in the coming years pursuant to the North Korea Human Rights Act of 2004. The U.S. also could designate North Korean persons outside North Korea and their foreign enablers for serious human rights violations and censorship pursuant to Section 304(b)(2) of the North Korea Sanctions and Policy Act. For example, with respect to the recent assassination of Kim Jong Nam, the designation of the former North Korean Ambassador to Malaysia, Kang Chul, and his staff, is warranted for their role in facilitating "serious human rights abuses by the Government of North Korea."

Moreover, Congress should publicly and repeatedly call on Pyongyang to tear down the walls of the nation's horrific political prisoner concentration camps. To date, no U.S. or South Korean president has ever made such a basic demand, out of fear of derailing the moribund-if not already-ossified nuclear talks with the Kim regime. Congress could encourage President Trump to call on Pyongyang to release all political prisoners. A firm, public stand by President Trump may not deter all third-country entities from engaging in shady deals with Pyongyang or move the Kim regime to close down its vast network of gulags. But it will raise cost of collusion and continued crimes against humanity.

III. Conclusion

To forge the future with proactive coercive diplomacy—one that employs targeted financial sanctions and multi-faceted information dissemination into the North—in tandem with conventional diplomacy and military deterrence offers hope. To remain reactive or return to the failed North Korea policies of the past will only give the Kim regime more time to perfect its nuclear arsenal while millions of ordinary North Koreans remain abused by the state. Coddling Pyongyang will ensure complete failure and beckon calamity.

The lessons of the past should not be supplanted by unfounded visions of the future. If the United States were truly intent on leaning on China to rein in Pyongyang's nuclear and missile programs, it should act beyond mere moral suasion. Instead, give the Chinese a credible stake in the matter—an economic stake in the protection of the integrity of the international financial system that may be adversely affected by continuing to support the Kim regime. But until then, the

---

[11] Broadcasting Board of Governors, "Fiscal Year 2017 Congressional Budget Request," 130, 135-136. https://www.bbg.gov/wp-content/media/2011/12/FY-2017-Budget-Submission.pdf

Chinese will stay the course they've been on the past sixty years. The Chinese leadership will put up with a recalcitrant Pyongyang, make platitudes about upholding peace and stability in the region, and counsel Washington on the need for patience and dialogue as North Korea continues to march to its own drumbeat of internal repression, periodic provocations, proliferation, weapons tests, and nuclear blackmail.

Whether the political situation in South Korea today turns into an opportunity or liability largely depends on actions by the U.S. Regime collapse in a democracy won't bring down the entire political order, but it may lead to the revival of failed policies. On the other hand, regime collapse in a dictatorship may well mean the destruction of the existing system and the launch of a new legal order, which, in the North Korean context, may mean liberation for millions.

This should be the tacit goal of the U.S. Unless Kim Jong Un faces the specter of regime collapse, he will neither disarm nor free his downtrodden people. The change in government in Seoul this spring neither precludes nor triggers one in the North. Still, it may yet accelerate the latter by showing the long-suffering people in the North the immutable truth—that the voice of the people sometimes does morph into Vox Dei; and that the voice of the people, inaudible and inarticulate as it may be, can in both democracies and tyrannies alike, effect, change, and even *end* regimes.

The United States is uniquely well-positioned to accelerate that eventuality.

Mr. Yоно. Dr. Lee, I appreciate it. And I almost opened announcing you, how poetic and eloquent your writing was, and I wished I had.

Mr. Ruggiero, go ahead.

STATEMENT OF MR. ANTHONY RUGGIERO, SENIOR FELLOW, FOUNDATION FOR DEFENSE OF DEMOCRACIES

Mr. RUGGIERO. Thank you. Thank you, Chairman Yoho, Ranking Member Sherman, and distinguished members of the subcommittee. Thank you for the opportunity to testify today.

The Kim family dynasty continues to threaten the United States and our allies in Japan and South Korea with its nuclear program.

Secretary of State Tillerson's trip to Asia last week noted that all options are on the table, including the military option. This is the right approach. We must take a page out of the Iran economic warfare effort and ensure that every option is considered.

We should not kid ourselves. North Korea tested a four-missile salvo as preparation for a military conflict, and we need to be equally prepared. U.S.-South Korea military exercises are crucial to our preparedness. We should also look to increase military cooperation with Japan and South Korea, and even explore the possibility of stationing additional military assets in the region.

In addition to military deterrence, we must use all other levers of American power. This includes offensive and defensive cyber warfare strategies.

We must also include robust sanctions. The good news is we have a successful template, the Iran sanctions regime. I had the privilege to work on both North Korea and Iran sanctions programs at the State and Treasury Departments. We understood the gravity of the situation, and we engaged in robust economic and financial warfare to address Tehran's direct threat to the United States. We need to replicate that approach with North Korea.

The U.N. report released last month detailed the stunning finding that the SWIFT electronic banking network was providing financial messaging services to North Korean banks, including ones designated for proliferation activities. The report suggests that SWIFT will finally halt its services to North Korean banks, and it is long overdue. North Korea's access to the SWIFT system is a symptom of a larger problem: Indifference toward Pyongyang's financial activities. With extremely limited exceptions, North Korea should not have access to the international financial system. We cannot trust that Pyongyang's financial transactions are legitimate. It is, therefore, our responsibility to block this access.

To this end, we must act against Chinese banks that facilitate North Korean financial transactions, just as we acted against several European banks that helped Iran evade sanctions. In fact, the U.S. fined these banks over $12 billion collectively for sanctions violations. Chinese banks continue to be the financial lifeline for North Korea, and we have not done enough to cut off this flow of money.

Two stories are instructive here: First, in September 2016, the Justice Department revealed that China-North Korea scheme that provided Kim's regime access to the American banking system. A Chinese company and four Chinese nationals created 22 front companies, and Chinese banks were used to conduct transactions for U.S. sanctioned North Korean bank. No Chinese bank was sanctioned or fined for this activity, and this activity was allowed to take place for 6 years.

Second, in the December 2015 trial of Chinpo Shipping in Singapore revealed that a Bank of China representative suggested that the company could transact in dollars, so long as it concealed references to North Korean vessels and wire transfers. Bank of China should have been fined by the U.S., even if it was limited to a single overzealous employee. The U.S. must clarify that this conduct is unacceptable.

North Korea is a global foreign policy challenge. North Korea proliferated ballistic missiles to Iran, Syria, and other countries, and secretly built a nuclear reactor in Syria in a location that has since fallen to ISIS. The reactor was destroyed in 2007, reportedly by Israel. There have also been unconfirmed reports that Israel destroyed missiles destined for Hezbollah.

A February 2016 CRS report on Iran-North Korea nexus showed that the ballistic missile relationship is significant and meaningful. The concern was so serious, that the Obama administration sanctioned Iran the day after the nuclear deal was implemented. In the accompanying explanation, Treasury revealed that senior Iranian officials were working with North Korea for several years and had traveled to Pyongyang to work on a component of North Korea's missile system.

Pyongyang will soon have in its possession a nuclear-armed ballistic missile capable of hitting North America. This deserves increasingly harsh responses from Washington.

Similarly, China is deserving of increasingly harsh U.S. responses. Beijing is critical of any effort to increase sanctions against North Korea. We should not let it stand in our way, as it has been doing.

Sanctions against North Korea and China are the only peaceful means for coercing the regime and are, for that reason, indispensable, but we must be prepared to deploy a full range of other measures to deter the threat.

And I look forward to addressing your questions.

[The prepared statement of Mr. Ruggiero follows:]

40

House Foreign Affairs Committee
Subcommittee on Asia and the Pacific

Pressuring North Korea:
Evaluating Options

ANTHONY RUGGIERO

Senior Fellow
Foundation for Defense of Democracies

Washington, DC
March 21, 2017

www.defenddemocracy.org

Anthony Ruggiero   March 21, 2017

Introduction

Chairman Yoho, Ranking Member Sherman, and distinguished members of this subcommittee, thank you for the opportunity to address you today on this important issue.

My testimony will outline four core elements to create a more effective North Korea policy, myths on North Korean sanctions, review North Korean sanctions evasion, and provide recommendations for Congress and the Trump administration.

The Kim family dynasty continues its 25-year drive to develop a nuclear weapon that it has already used to threaten the United States and our allies in Japan and South Korea. The last three U.S. presidents, Republicans and Democrats, were unable to develop an effective strategy to prevent North Korea from acquiring a nuclear weapon. Now Kim Jong Un has threatened to test an intercontinental ballistic missile (ICBM) that could reach the United States, and last month tested a solid propellant ballistic missile and killed his half-brother with nerve agent in a Malaysian airport. Earlier this month he simulated an attack on a base in Japan. We know that North Korea has proliferated ballistic missiles to Iran, Syria, and other nations, and secretly built a nuclear reactor in Syria in a location that has since fallen to ISIS.[1] Pyongyang is likely to proliferate the technology it develops to other rogue regimes, such as Iran.

One expert has predicted that North Korea could have an operational ICBM by 2020.[2] It is plausible, even likely, that by 2020, the regime will have a miniaturized nuclear device that could survive reentry on an ICBM, or may even have such a capability already.[3]

Meanwhile, South Korea may soon elect a president who once questioned the deployment of THAAD – a U.S. anti-ballistic missile system designed to shoot down short-, medium-, and intermediate-range ballistic missiles in their terminal phase.[4] Advisors to the candidate, Moon Jae In, last week suggested that the next South Korean president should review THAAD's deployment.[5] Moon has also advocated negotiations with North Korea that would include offering the regime financial inducements that would undermine the financial pressure of U.N. and U.S. sanctions, and which could violate recent U.N. Security Council resolutions.[6] This scenario is concerning, as Washington has tried to alter Pyongyang's behavior through economic engagement for 25 years, as well as disarming it through bilateral and multilateral negotiations, resulting in

---

[1] David Albright, Serena Kelleher-Vergantini, and Sarah Burkhard, "Syria's Unresolved Nuclear Issues Reemerge in Wake of ISIL Advance and Ongoing Civil War," *Institute for Science and International Security*, June 30, 2015. (http://isis-online.org/uploads/isis-reports/documents/Syria_June_30_2015_Final.pdf)

[2] John Schilling, "North Korea's Large Rocket Engine Test: A Significant Step Forward for Pyongyang's ICBM Program," *38 North*, April 11, 2016. (http://38north.org/2016/04/schilling041116/)

[3] Jeffrey Lewis, "North Korea's Nuke Program Is Way More Sophisticated Than You Think," *Foreign Policy*, September 9, 2016. (http://foreignpolicy.com/2016/09/09/north-koreas-nuclear-program-is-way-more-sophisticated-and-dangerous-than-you-think/)

[4] James Griffiths and Joshua Berlinger, "What is THAAD?" *CNN*, September 9, 2016. (http://www.cnn.com/2016/07/13/asia/what-is-thaad/)

[5] Yeganeh Torbati and James Pearson, "Top South Korean presidential candidate would review missile defense process: advisors," *Reuters*, March 17, 2017. (http://www.reuters.com/article/us-southkorea-china-thaad-idUSKBN16O0ZF)

[6] Kent Boydston, "Moon Jae-In on North-South Integration," *North Korea: Witness to Transformation*, September 8, 2015. (https://piie.com/blogs/north-korea-witness-transformation/moon-jae-north-south-integration)

three separate agreements with Pyongyang to freeze or dismantle its nuclear weapons. This approach has completely failed.

The approach outlined below preserves U.S. dedication to the denuclearization of the Korean Peninsula while acknowledging that North Korea is not ready to negotiate away its nuclear weapons. Nonetheless, the Kim family must know that the United States will not accept it as a nuclear state or back down against its aggressive actions.

In my testimony before the full committee last month, I reviewed the impact of the North Korea Sanctions and Policy Enhancement Act (NKSPEA) of 2016.[7] While the law was a significant step forward, there is more that the U.S. should do. The law is largely responsible for nearly doubling the number of designations since March 2016, but 88 percent of those were persons inside North Korea, which does not address Pyongyang's international business.

Four Core Policy Elements

The Trump administration can return to a more effective North Korea policy with four core policy elements.

1. <u>Tough talk, no negotiations</u>. Kim has no present interest in giving up his nuclear weapons, and would see renewed negotiations with the West over his arsenal as an opportunity to buy time or extract new concessions. But it is useful to tell North Korea directly or in a multilateral format that the U.S. will increase sanctions and sanctions implementation, continue military exercises, and place additional military assets in the region. Pyongyang needs to know what to expect in response to its continued destabilizing behavior. It is also essential that Pyongyang understand that it has a non-violent, diplomatic exit strategy that is vastly preferable to the alternatives. Additionally, it is crucial that any discussions be held in close consultation with U.S. allies, including reassuring them that it will not abandon or bargain away their interests.

   Two common North Korea policy suggestions are negotiating a freeze of its nuclear and missile programs and agreeing to a peace treaty to formally end the Korean War.[8] These, however, do not address the real issue: that North Korea is unwilling to denuclearize. The U.S. has tried freezes before: in 1994, 2005, 2007, and 2012. The Leap Day deal only last two weeks before North Korea was back to its provocations. A peace treaty in the face of North Korea's aggressive actions and Beijing's sanctions against South Korea over THAAD would be poor policy.[9] North Korea will simply pocket all the benefits from negotiating a freeze or treaty without any actual drawdown to its nuclear and missile programs. Beijing and Pyongyang will then likely insist on the reduction or complete

[7] Anthony Ruggiero. "Countering the North Korean Threat: New Steps in U.S. Policy," *Testimony Before House Foreign Affairs Committee*, February 7, 2017.

[8] Leon Sigal, "Why Trump should strike a deal with North Korea," *CNN*, March 7, 2017.
(http://www.cnn.com/2017/03/06/opinions/north-korea-talks/); Ann Wright, "It's time to for the U.S. to negotiate a peace treaty with North Korea," *NK News*, March 16, 2017. (https://www.nknews.org/2017/03/its-time-for-the-u-s-to-sign-a-peace-treaty-with-north-korea/)

[9] David Straub, "The North Korean nuclear freeze mirage," *The Hill*, January 27, 2017.
(http://thehill.com/blogs/congress-blog/foreign-policy/316488-the-north-korean-nuclear-freeze-mirage)

withdrawal of U.S. troops from South Korea and possibly Japan. These policy options are not feasible at this time, and robust new sanctions and implementation of existing sanctions are better options for moving forward.

2. Get tough with China. In 2016, a ground-breaking study by C4ADS and South Korea's Asan Institute for Policy Studies documented how China is turning a blind eye to North Korea's nuclear and missile programs.[10] Beijing said it would end imports of North Korean coal,[11] but after a similar ban last April, China imported over $800 million of North Korean coal. China must be treated as part of the problem until it shows that it can be part of the solution.

    The Trump administration has vowed to get tough with Beijing. This is an important place to start, and a smarter policy than that taken by Presidents Clinton, Bush, and Obama – all of whom tried softer approaches on dealing with China on North Korea issue. Each of these efforts produced agreements of limited value. For Clinton and Bush, post-deal implementation focused more on preserving the deals than holding China or North Korea to their commitments.

3. Support key allies in the region. Washington should work with South Korea and Japan, and also Australia and other Asian allies, to use tools or other mechanisms to stymie North Korea's proliferation activities. This could include the Proliferation Security Initiative, a coalition of 105 nations dedicated to interdicting materials used in weapons of mass destruction – The U.S. should also conduct additional high-profile military exercises with its allies as a deterrent to North Korea. We must reassure South Korea amid China's efforts to intimidate it into canceling the deployment of the U.S. Terminal High Altitude Area Defense (THAAD) missile defense system.

4. Introduce new sanctions on North Korea and strengthen existing ones. Senator Cory Gardner (R-CO) on January 2 noted the importance of secondary sanctions and other measures to utilize the country's cyber activities to ensure there are consequences for North Korea and those who help it violate U.N. sanctions or U.S. law.[12] I discuss specific sanctions recommendations for Congress and the Trump administration later in my testimony.

Myths on North Korea Sanctions

Understanding the utility of sanctions as part of a broader, coherent North Korea policy is often clouded by myths about the country's history. It is common for scholars and journalists to note that years of strong sanctions against North Korea have failed. It is true that thus far, sanctions

---

[10] "In China's Shadow," *The Asan Institute for Policy Studies and C4ADS*, August 2016. (https://static1.squarespace.com/static/566cf8b4d8af107232d5358a/t/57dfc74acd0f68d629357306/1474291539480/In+China%27s+Shadow.pdf)

[11] Anthony Ruggiero, "China's 'ban' on North Korean coal isn't the tough stance it seems," *The Hill*, February 28, 2017. (http://thehill.com/blogs/pundits-blog/foreign-policy/321552-dont-be-fooled-chinas-ban-on-north-korean-coal-isnt-the)

[12] Cory Gardner, "Why Donald Trump should make North Korea a top priority," *CNN*, January 2, 2017. (http://www.cnn.com/2017/01/02/opinions/trump-north-korea-priority-opinion/)

Anthony Ruggiero   March 21, 2017

have not achieved the U.S. objective of disarming North Korea, but it is not true that sanctions have been strong or well-enforced, or that they cannot work. The most prevalent myths include the following:

1. Myth #1: North Korea is the world's most-sanctioned country. Despite North Korea's provocations over the last 25 years, the United States has demonstrated extraordinary restraint in sanctioning the country. A U.S. president only gave the Treasury secretary comprehensive authority to designate North Korean officials and party members in January 2015, and sanctions began to accelerate only in March 2016, after a new sanctions law went into effect. To date, designations on Pyongyang lag far behind those placed on Iran before the 2015 nuclear deal. The number and timing of designations reveal the commitment Washington has shown on sanctioning North Korea relative to other countries. Today, U.S. designations on North Korean are on par with those against Zimbabwe. [13] Washington still has far more sanctions against Iran and Russia than against the hermit kingdom.

2. Myth #2: North Korea is isolated financially. North Korea consistently obscures its access to the international financial system using non-traceable front companies, a practice that the Treasury Department has called "a threat to the integrity of the U.S. financial system."[14] Such actions put banks at a disadvantage, especially when governments are unwilling to identify these companies. The U.N. earlier this month noted that North Korea used foreign banks to process transactions through accounts in the U.S. and Europe.[15] Treasury similarly discovered that designated North Korean banks have conducted financial transactions through the American banking system. The Justice Department also found that from August 2009 to September 2015, Chinese nationals had used 22 front companies to open Chinese bank accounts to conduct dollar financial transactions through the U.S. financial system when completing sales to Pyongyang.[16]

3. Myth #3: the U.S. will run out of North Korea designations. The number of North Korea designations nearly doubled over the last year. Washington has finally directly sanctioned the country's leader Kim Jong Un, numerous government ministries, shipping companies, seven banks, and the national airline. Unfortunately, these designations did not touch North Korean international business ties. Despite abundant evidence of deceptive Chinese financial practices, Washington has not designated, fined, or investigated a single Chinese bank for illicit North Korean activity. Washington may believe that it cannot sanction

---

[13] Joshua Stanton, "You'd be surprised how much tougher our Zimbabwe and Belarus sanctions are than our North Korea sanctions," One Free Korea, July 15, 2014.
(http://freekorea.us/?s=zimbabwe#sthash.uv4SyGfI.MhSXDHoI.dpbs)
[14] U.S. Department of the Treasury, Financial Crimes Enforcement Network, "Finding that the Democratic People's Republic of Korea is a Jurisdiction of Primary Money Laundering Concern," 81 Federal Register 35441, June 2, 2016. (https://www.fincen.gov/sites/default/files/shared/2016-13038(DPRK_Finding).pdf)
[15] United Nations Security Council, "Report of the Panel of Experts established pursuant to resolution 1874 (2009)," S/2017/150, February 27, 2017. (http://undocs.org/S/2017/150)
[16] U.S. Department of Justice, Press Release, "Four Chinese Nationals and China-Based Company Charged with Using Front Companies to Evade U.S. Sanctions Targeting North Korea's Nuclear Weapons and Ballistic Missile Programs," September 26, 2016. (https://www.justice.gov/opa/pr/four-chinese-nationals-and-china-based-company-charged-using-front-companies-evade-us)

Beijing without jeopardizing other priorities such as the Iran deal, but the failure to sanction Chinese financial institutions has drastically reduced the efficacy of both American and U.N. sanctions against North Korea.

4. Myth #4: China will not respond to pressure over North Korea. Conventional wisdom says Beijing will shelter North Korea from international sanctions at all cost.[17] That is not necessarily true. Treasury sanctioned North Korea's Foreign Trade Bank in 2013 because it was facilitating transactions on behalf of actors linked to Pyongyang's proliferation network.[18] Two months later, the Bank of China sent the Foreign Trade Bank a notice closing its account.[19] When Washington moved against Chinese nationals aiding a designated North Korean bank in September 2016, Beijing arrested 10 people and froze the assets of those involved.[20] When Pyongyang threatens Chinese economic interests, Beijing can tighten its lifeline to North Korea, even moving against its own citizens who had likely been authorized to trade with the country.

North Korean Sanctions Evasion

The United Nations issued its annual report earlier this month on North Korea, revealing numerous sanctions violations and confirming widespread suspicions that international sanctions on Pyongyang are poorly enforced. As the report notes, North Korea consistently obscures its access to the international financial system. The report also warns that these efforts generate significant revenue for the Kim regime, most of it denominated in dollars, euros, and Chinese renminbi. North Korea's reliance on the international financial system is concerning, but also provides the U.S. leverage to address Pyongyang's illicit activities.

The U.N. report also detailed the stunning finding that SWIFT provides financial messaging services to North Korean banks, including designated ones, although on March 7 *The Wall Street Journal* reported that SWIFT would stop providing its services to banks in the country.[21]

This was not SWIFT's first dance with rogue regimes; in 2012 it provided these services to Iranian banks, including the Central Bank of Iran. SWIFT finally acted against Tehran's banks,

---

[17] Joel Wit and Richard Sokolsky, "The Art of a Deal with North Korea, *Politico*, January 24, 2017. (http://www.politico.com/magazine/story/2017/01/the-art-of-a-deal-with-north-korea-214686)

[18] U.S. Department of the Treasury, "Press Release: Treasury Sanctions Bank and Official Linked to North Korean Weapons of Mass Destruction Programs," March 11, 2013. (https://www.treasury.gov/press-center/press-releases/Pages/jl1876.aspx)

[19] Simon Rabinovitch and Simon Mundy, "China reduces banking lifeline to N Korea." *Financial Times*, May 7, 2013. (https://www.ft.com/content/a7154272-b702-11e2-a249-00144feabdc0)

[20] U.S. Department of Justice, Press Release, "Four Chinese Nationals and China-Based Company Charged with Using Front Companies to Evade U.S. Sanctions Targeting North Korea's Nuclear Weapons and Ballistic Missile Programs," September 26, 2016. (https://www.justice.gov/opa/pr/four-chinese-nationals-and-china-based-company-charged-using-front-companies-evade-us); Elizabeth Shim, "China arrests more than 10 business executives for North Korea trade," UPI, September 21, 2016. (http://www.upi.com/Top_News/World-News/2016/09/21/China-arrests-more-than-10-business-executives-for-North-Korea-trade/1531474469593/)

[21] Jay Solomon. "Swift Banking System Bars North Korean Banks." *The Wall Street Journal*, March 7, 2017. (https://www.wsj.com/articles/swift-banking-system-bars-several-north-korean-banks-1488937466)

Anthony Ruggiero   March 21, 2017

including those designated for proliferation and terrorism, after Congress began consideration of sanctions legislation prohibiting the practice.[22]

SWIFT claims that provided its services to U.N.-designated North Korean banks after receiving authorization from Belgium. Belgium should not have provided the authorizations in the first place, and the U.N. noted that they were violations of its sanctions. These authorizations also likely violated the discretionary sanctions in the North Korea Sanctions and Policy Enhancement Act of 2016 against knowingly providing financial support for U.N.-designated persons.[23]

North Korea's SWIFT access is a symptom of a larger problem: malaise toward Pyongyang's financial activities. The Justice Department in September 2016 revealed a China-North Korea scheme that provided the Kim regime access to the American banking system over a six-year period.[24] No Chinese bank was sanctioned or fined for this activity. The North Korean bank at the center of this network is one of the U.N.-designated banks on SWIFT that were noted in the U.N. report.

In the December 2015 trial of Chinpo Shipping in Singapore, a Bank of China representative suggested transactions in dollars would be successful if the company removed references to North Korean vessels in wire transfers.[25] Bank of China should have been fined by the U.S. even if such remarks were limited to a single overzealous employee, and the U.S. must clarify that this conduct is unacceptable.

The U.N. has said, and Reuters confirmed, North Korea's efforts to sell military equipment from a front company purportedly in Malaysia.[26] This network and its banks have not been sanctioned.

Recommendations for Congress

1. <u>Mandate additional resources to address North Korea's activities.</u> The North Korea Sanctions and Policy Enhancement Act of 2016 is a comprehensive law that provides a myriad of tools for the Trump administration to address the North Korean threat. It is important that Congress continue to address additional areas through legislation in the same overwhelmingly bipartisan nature, signaling to North Korea and China that focus on this

---

[22] Rick Gladstone and Stephen Castle, "Global Network Expels as Many as 30 of Iran's Banks in Move to Isolate Its Economy," *The New York Times*, March 15, 2012. (http://www.nytimes.com/2012/03/16/world/middleeast/crucial-communication-network-expelling-iranian-banks.html); *Reuters*, "Payments system SWIFT to expel Iranian banks Saturday," March 15, 2012. (http://www.reuters.com/article/us-nuclear-iran-idUSBRE82E15M20120315)
[23] North Korea Sanctions and Policy Enhancement Act of 2016, Pub. L. No. 114-122, 130 Stat. 93, codified as amended at 114 U.S.C. §201. (https://www.congress.gov/114/bills/hr757/BILLS-114hr757enr.pdf)
[24] U.S. Department of Justice, Press Release, "Four Chinese Nationals and China-Based Company Charged with Using Front Companies to Evade U.S. Sanctions Targeting North Korea's Nuclear Weapons and Ballistic Missile Programs," September 26, 2016. (https://www.justice.gov/opa/pr/four-chinese-nationals-and-china-based-company-charged-using-front-companies-evade-us)
[25] Andrea Berger, "Thanks to the Banks: Counter-Proliferation Finance and the Chinpo Shipping Case," *38 North*, December 16, 2015. (http://38north.org/2015/12/aberger121615/)
[26] United Nations Security Council, "Report of the Panel of Experts established pursuant to resolution 1874 (2009)," S/2017/150, February 27, 2017. (http://undocs.org/S/2017/150); James Pearson and Rozanna Latiff, "North Korea spy agency runs arms operation out of Malaysia, U.N. says," Reuters, February 27, 2017. (http://uk.reuters.com/article/uk-northkorea-malaysia-arms-insight-idUKKBN1650YG)

issue will continue. Throughout my testimony, I have detailed the challenge we face with an adversary that seems to be one step ahead of us. Our entire approach to the North Korea issue needs to change. One area Congress can address immediately is providing additional resources to the Treasury Department, Justice Department, Intelligence Community, and other government agencies to investigate violations of the NKSPEA.

2. Restrict travel to North Korea. I noted in my testimony last month to the full committee that the State Department's enhanced travel warnings mandated by the NKSPEA are important to protecting the safety of U.S. nationals.[27] Banning tourist travel would also amplify the effectiveness of the recent designation of North Korea's national flag carrier, Air Koryo, and deny Pyongyang another source of hard currency. By law, the president does not have the authority to ban transactions incident to travel to, from, or within North Korea without further action by Congress.[28] Congress, however, could pass legislation authorizing the president to restrict travel to North Korea by requiring licenses for such transactions. The benefit of this licensing system is that it would allow the United States to screen and be aware of all U.S. persons in North Korea. The licensing system could also have exceptions for U.S. government travel and private trips associated with humanitarian missions. This action would restrict tourist travel to North Korea.

3. Investigate China. The Treasury and Justice Departments' actions in late September 2016 showed a troubling pattern of Chinese persons assisting North Korean-designated persons, including through the U.S. financial system. These transactions lasted six years, to September 2015, making it hard to believe the Chinese government regulators were unaware of this conduct. It is important that Congress understand the extent of China's efforts, or lack thereof, to combat money laundering, sanctions violations, and proliferation financing. I recommend that new legislation include specific sections on North Korea's network within China. It should also address the broader issue of Chinese support for, and harboring of, North Korean nationals involved in prohibited conduct. In particular, the report could also focus on whether the financial institutions involved should have been designated or subjected to secondary sanctions.

4. Prohibit Relationships with North Korean Banks: SWIFT's action to stop providing financial messaging services to North Korean banks was important and overdue. But it is important for Congress to be clear that any business, with few exceptions, with North Korean banks is unacceptable. The trade-off must be clear: continuing business with North Korea will bring significant consequences. The United Nations Security Council Resolutions has progressively tightened restrictions on relationships with North Korean banks. However, the U.N. reported the use of SWIFT and front companies for U.N -

---

[27] The State Department "strongly urges U.S. citizens to avoid all travel to North Korea/the Democratic People's Republic of Korea (DPRK) due to the serious risk of arrest and long-term detention under North Korea's system of law enforcement, which imposes unduly harsh sentences, including for actions that in the United States would not be considered crimes and which threaten U.S. citizen detainees with being treated in accordance with "wartime law of the DPRK." U.S. Department of State, "North Korea Travel Warning." November 9, 2016. (https://travel.state.gov/content/passports/en/alertswarnings/north-korea-travel-warning.html)

[28] International Emergency Economic Powers Act of 1977, Pub. L. 95-223, 91 Stat. 1625, codified as amended at 95 U.S.C. §103(b)(4).

48

Anthony Ruggiero   March 21, 2017

designated North Korean banks. The U.S. should play a leadership role in adopting sanctions against those who provide any services to North Korean banks.

5. Extend the North Korea Human Rights Act: The Kim family regime's treatment of its own people is appalling, and Beijing's willingness to excuse its actions is disappointing. The United States must lead the effort to promote information flow into North Korea and hold the hermit kingdom accountable for its actions. China has prevented the U.N. from sending North Korea's case to the International Criminal Court. But Congressional action to extend this important law will keep focus on the issue and ensure the Trump administration makes it a priority in discussions with Pyongyang and Beijing.

Recommendations for the Trump Administration

1. Make significant changes to our North Korea sanctions efforts. North Korea represents a direct threat to the United States and our allies, and we must radically change our approach to North Korea sanctions efforts. All remaining North Korean banks should be designated immediately. A senior official from the Treasury Department should make clear in a major speech or Congressional testimony that Washington will enforce requirements on financial institutions. These will help those institutions know their customer, enabling the use of sanctions against those who do not comply.

   President Trump should direct the attorney general and Treasury secretary to jointly investigate the Treasury and Justice actions in late September 2016, and the Bank of China for its 2013 transactions on behalf of Chinpo Shipping.[29] The Treasury secretary should take strong action against any bank that continues to provide direct or indirect financial services to North Korean banks.

2. Designate additional persons before the next North Korean provocation. The United States has a tendency to engage in a provocation-response cycle in response to North Korea's provocative behavior. This approach is dangerous, as it suggests that Pyongyang is only a threat when it engages in provocations. In fact, North Korea is a threat to the United States and our allies every day that it continues development of nuclear weapons, means of delivery, and proliferation activities. Part of this new approach would include investigating China-North Korea activities and using the North Korea Sanctions and Policy Enhancement Act of 2016 to designate persons, including Chinese financial institutions, with sanctions and secondary sanctions. A critical aspect of this approach is the designation of North Korean front companies on a regular basis. Financial institutions can be an ally in the effort to stop North Korea's activities, but that can only happen if there is a regular designation process that exposes North Korea's efforts to compromise the financial system through front companies.

3. Enhance diplomatic efforts to implement sanctions. The United States is uniquely positioned to lead a diplomatic effort to implement existing sanctions and create the environment for new multilateral sanctions. These would be done through the U.N. or with

---

[29] Andrea Berger, "Thanks to the Banks: Counter-Proliferation Finance and the Chinpo Shipping Case," *38 North*, December 16, 2015. (http://38north.org/2015/12/aberger121615/)

Anthony Ruggiero   March 21, 2017

international coalitions concerned with the prevention of money laundering, smuggling, proliferation, and human trafficking. The U.N. Panel of Experts has consistently called out the poor implementation of U.N. sanctions already in place. The United States, particularly its Special Representative for North Korea Policy, could lead that effort.[30] It is also important that these efforts reinforce the idea that while a significant percentage of North Korea's trade is with China, Pyongyang has other economically important and dangerous relationships with other states. The U.S. government must be properly organized, staffed, and resourced for this mission, and it is imperative that North Korea be given the highest priority when it comes to diplomatic engagement and sanctions investigations.

4. Increase engagement at the United Nations. A general sanctions rule is that the United States leads while other states and multilateral bodies (such as the U.N. and European Union) follow. That rule is instructive here, where Washington must use all of its sanctions and investigative tools, including the resources of non-governmental organizations, to expose North Korea's illicit network. The United States could use the information it acquires to host information sessions for interested delegations. The U.S. should also increase its support to the U.N. Panel of Experts, including by providing it more information about the status and location of key North Korean networks and assets.

Conclusion

North Korea is an extraordinary foreign-policy challenge. Pyongyang's provocations, which will soon lead to a nuclear-armed ballistic missile capable of hitting North America, deserve increasingly harsh responses from Washington.[31] And while China is critical to any effort to increase sanctions against North Korea, America has in the past sought Beijing's cooperation at the U.N. – a strategy that failed completely. If Washington wants to be serious about sanctions, it must acknowledge that China is part of the North Korea problem until Beijing demonstrates otherwise. Sanctions against North Korea and China are the only peaceful means for coercing the regime, and are for that reason indispensable.

On behalf of the Foundation for Defense of Democracies, I thank you again for inviting me to testify and I look forward to addressing your questions.

---

[30] United Nations Security Council. "Report of the Panel of Experts established pursuant to resolution 1874 (2009)." S/2016/157. February 24, 2016. (http://www.un.org/ga/search/view_doc.asp?symbol=S/2016/157)
[31] John Schilling, "North Korea's Large Rocket Engine Test: A Significant Step Forward for Pyongyang's ICBM Program," 38 North. April 11, 2016. (http://38north.org/2016/04/schilling041116/)

Mr. YOHO. Thank you all for great testimonies, and we look forward to some spirited talks here.

Bringing out the information, and it perplexes me, what does North Korea want? I know people say they want legitimacy of a nuclear power. Is that correct?

But then what? If they become a nuclear power, are they going to play nicer? And I think—I don't see a good end stage to the direction they are heading into. I don't know what their fear is.

Mr. Ruggiero, what is their underlying theme other than they want legitimacy as a nuclear power?

Mr. RUGGIERO. Sure. I believe they want a nuclear weapon so that they can coerce the United States into what they want us to do, which is to acknowledge them as a nuclear weapon state. I think that is the fallacy of the discussion of a peace treaty as one of the prerequisites for solving this nuclear issue.

Mr. YOHO. And I see that as a false narrative, because even if they get to that stage, which we all think they are pretty close to that, if they get to that stage, the behavior, I don't see changing.

Dr. Lee, do you see their behavior changing in North Korea?

Mr. LEE. No, Mr. Chairman. It sounds rather absurd, but North Korea, I believe, has a long-term strategic goal in mind. It is a revisionist, revolutionary state. The North Korean Communist revolution still rages on in the eyes of the North Korean leadership.

De-nuclearization would basically mean that North Korea would give up on its own raison d'etre, claiming to be the sole legitimate Korean state, the perennial fear of being absorbed by that other Korean state. That is an existential challenge. So North Korea, by demonstrating to the United States and to the world a credible capability of combining a nuclear warhead with a long-range missile that can hit all parts of the United States, then North Korea's leverage, its ability to resort to nuclear blackmail, extortion on all kinds of issues.

Mr. YOHO. But in the 21st century, I mean, that is just a nonstarter with the amount of nations with nuclear weapons, that I would think—and I know going through vet school, common sense was not common, one of my professors said, because if it was, everybody would have it. You know, I don't see anybody wanting to invade North Korea. You would think they would want to become part of the world community and start doing what is best for their people.

I am going to go to Mr. Klingner and ask you with the North Korea Sanctions and Policy Enhancement Act of 2016, which I am glad President Obama started to put the pressure on North Korea, I feel it was a little late, but I am glad it was there, what can we do so that this administration doesn't back off from that. I am glad to hear the strong language from Mr. Tillerson that we continue down this road. Is there anything else that you would recommend that we throw in there, whether it is more sanctions on Chinese companies or any country that has business dealings with North Korea?

Mr. KLINGNER. Yes. Thank you, sir. On your first point, their nuclear weapons serve a number of purposes, including a military purpose. We often see it only as a signal or a message. But, when Kim Jong Un came into power, he directed his military to come up with a new war plan to be able to occupy the Korean Peninsula within 7 days. That would require them to go nuclear early on. We have seen the development of capabilities to fulfill that plan. Last year, when they conducted missile launches, they said it was to practice nuclear air bursts over South Korean ports through which U.S. reinforcements would come through, and they had a graphic for it. Recently, with the salvo of four missiles, they said this was practicing an attack on U.S. bases in Japan. So they want that capability, and the ICBM is to be able to hit the United States with a nuclear weapon. They have been having this quest for decades. Now, that doesn't mean they are going to wake up someday and just start a war, but by having that capability, they see it as—another reason would be deterring U.S. military action. They would depict it as us unilaterally attacking out of the blue; we would see it as them preventing us from responding to a tactical or operational-level North Korean attack.

And also, as Mr. Ruggiero said, it is coercive diplomacy, not only acknowledgement of them as a nuclear weapon state, but also to intimidate South Korea into providing benefits or not responding to actions of North Korea.

Opening up North Korea goes against what they want. They have said they do not want to allow the contagion of outside influence, they need to keep it out, because it would undermine the strength and legitimacy of the regime.

I think the North Korea Sanctions and Policy Enhancement Act was a superb step forward, not only in the measures it had, but the ability to try to induce the Obama administration to move forward on exercising the authorities it already had. So I hope the Trump administration will——

Mr. YOHO. I want to cut you off there. I have got one quick question for each of you. Would you recommend putting North Korea back on the State Sponsor of Terrorism? Mr. Klingner?

Mr. KLINGNER. Absolutely, sir.

Mr. YOHO. Dr. Lee?

Mr. LEE. Absolutely.

Mr. YOHO. Mr. Ruggiero?

Mr. RUGGIERO. Absolutely.

Mr. YOHO. Thank you. I am going to yield back and go to the ranking member, Mr. Sherman.

Mr. SHERMAN. You stole my question, but we got good answers.

The chairman says no one wants to invade North Korea. That is easy for us to say. I was here when Dick Cheney did want to invade North Korea, or at least put the kibosh on any nonaggression pact with North Korea, because he wanted to keep open the idea of using force to bring democracy to the northern part of that peninsula.

Who knows what we could have achieved in return for a nonaggression pact, but we very much wanted to keep all the—all options on the table, not to just to deal with North Korea's nuclear program, but to deal with them, their continued existence as a repressive state.

We have been hearing that for 20 years, we have had a failure. Yes, if you worry about our national security, but for 20 years, we have met the political needs of Washington and Wall Street. We do that by having a modest sanctions program that doesn't get Wall

Street out of joint or seriously affect trade with China, while maintaining maximum demands, because it is an affront to the foreign policy establishment here for us to ever talk about a slightly nuclear North Korea, or even to talk about giving them a peace treaty or nonaggression pact. So we have modest sanctions, maximum demands, no accomplishments, and we achieve all our domestic political objectives. I don't know if that is failure or not.

I do want to comment, as I have before, about civil defense. The purpose of civil defense appears to be, in this country, to calm our population. So back when Dana and I were kids, the population was concerned that we faced a massive Soviet nuclear hydrogen bomb threat, and they calmed us down a bit by having us hide under our desks. Not really anything effective.

Now, we might be faced with one atomic bomb. Civil defense might be successful. Immediate aid would come to any victimized city from all over the country. But in this case, not having civil defense calms our population, because if we had any civil defense, we would admit that there was a threat from North Korea, or there would be soon.

Mr. Ruggiero, I want to thank you for your comments about the trade between North Korea on the one hand, and the Shiite alliance, basically Assad and Iran, on the other. You pointed out how that has happened, continued to happen, and in light of Iran's additional money, or financial resources, could very well happen in the future.

Let's see. We have got—so the question here is, will modest sanctions achieve our maximalist aims?

I think, Dr. Lee, you have indicated that it goes to the very core of this regime to become a nuclear state. Would they give up on their nuclear program if that meant more luxury goods for their ruling elite, or would they be willing to suffer a 10 or 20 percent decline in luxury goods rather than give up their nuclear program? What is more important to them, Johnny Walker or nukes?

Mr. LEE. Continued supply of Johnny Walker, Mr. Congressman.

Mr. SHERMAN. Is more important to them than the nuclear program?

Mr. LEE. Well, all carrots eventually dry up. What would they do once they give up their nuclear weapons and no longer have that great lever with which to bully, extort the biggest powers in the world, including the United States? Depend on the goodwill of their neighbors? That would be a very poor policy.

I think there is no way that we can persuade, coerce the Kim regime to give up its nuclear weapons without, without putting sufficient pressure that makes them think that they are on the verge of political extinction.

Mr. SHERMAN. And a 20 percent decline in high quality Scotch, that would not put them on the verge of extinction, would it?

Mr. LEE. I believe it would be a big blow. So I think the ban, the U.N. Security Council ban on luxury goods exports to North Korea, that is an important component, but——

Mr. SHERMAN. So this regime is perhaps more fragile than I imagined.

Mr. LEE. Well, we have not tried really tough financial sanctions, as you know, Mr. Congressman. We know that North Korea is still dependent on the U.S. dollar system. It is their preferred currency of choice in international financial transactions. There is a lot that we can do to block—to designate North Korean entities and their enablers.

Mr. SHERMAN. Okay. So you are saying if we kept Chinese policy the same but were very effective in hurting the North Korean state, we could force a change in their behavior?

I will ask your two colleagues on either side whether they agree with that characterization.

Mr. KLINGNER. I would agree with you, sir, that weak sanctions are not effective, just as weakly enforcing the law in a city is not——

Mr. SHERMAN. But let's say we had sanctions that were just directed at North Korea, so they were effective in cutting 20 percent less Scotch, 20 percent less of all the other luxury goods, but China continued its current subsidies and trade with North Korea. Would that be enough to imperil the regime?

Mr. KLINGNER. Well, what I would argue is that we need to go after China as well. Anyone who violates U.S. laws and U.N. resolutions should not have immunity from our laws and the resolutions.

Mr. SHERMAN. I have gone way over time. I yield back. Thank you.

Mr. YOHO. Thank you, sir. I will go to our member from California, Mr. Rohrabacher.

Mr. ROHRABACHER. Well, again, let me note that the problem is not North Korea or North Koreans, it is this clique that seems— rather mentally ill clique that runs North Korea. The people of North Korea are victims. They are people who—perhaps many of them who don't even know they are victims. And perhaps our greatest strategy could be putting out an all-out effort to inform the people of North Korea exactly what is happening in the rest of the world, and how they are being short-changed and that their future is being robbed from their children by this current unscrupulous and brutal regime that controls their lives.

You know, one thing you could say, and this is a crazy regime, is the one—I was noting that this is one country, North Korea is one country that can accurately—it can accurately be said that its leaders have gone to the dogs. I mean, this is in—to think that a— now, is that an accurate report that this leader has sent people to be eaten by dogs, who had actually opposed his regime? Is that an accurate report?

Mr. KLINGNER. We don't think so. The story that Jang Song Thaek, his uncle, was eaten by dogs was started by a Chinese blogger, which then was picked up by Chinese media and then picked up by a foreign media. We think, instead, he was killed or executed with anti-aircraft artillery, as many others have been.

Mr. ROHRABACHER. Well, I see now—so he hasn't been eaten by the dogs, but he may well have been killed by being shot by anti-aircraft artillery. Hmm. All right. Gee, I am glad you said that. It really makes me feel better about the mental stability of those folks.

Now, it also was noted in there that we have a situation where South Korea, with such a vibrant economy and somewhat stability, at least, they have democratic processes going, we just had a leader removed from office and there wasn't blood shed.

I remember during the Reagan years, there was an economist that did a study all over the world, and Korea was one of them, where communism and free enterprise, or at least capitalism in some way, came together, and the only thing that separated the Communist area from the free enterprise area was a line, an arbitrary political line. So on both sides, they had the same kind of soil, same kind of weather. This economist noted for us in the White House, we asked to do this study, that the production of food and the production of wealth was so much greater on the non-Communist side of the border as compared to the Communist side of the border, which then we interpreted as meaning either—let's see. It was either that God exists and that God—it is either whether there is no God, or that God exists and he doesn't like Communists. The fact is that they can blame it—and a lot of our people try to blame our failures and different failures on global warming as well, but the fact is that you have these situations around the world where people who live in tyranny do not do well financially, which is, I would say, the Achilles heel of this regime, in that its people live in such poverty, that their children are smaller, and that there are all sorts of demonstrations of this.

I want to thank our witnesses today for giving us some specific things that we can do, especially in the economic arena, in terms of dealing with Chinese banks and making sure that we put the economic pressure on this regime.

Again, it is better to have no sanctions than to have soft sanctions. Teddy Roosevelt said, it is the greatest sin—the greatest sin is to hit someone softly. Either we are going to do this and we are going to get rid of that regime and work with the people of North Korea to free themselves, or we are not.

I would suggest that we should be working—and some of the suggestions you have given us today in terms of grabbing onto their economy so that that clique that runs North Korea cannot withstand the pressure that we have generated by this type of economic offensive on our side, that we take it and we do that seriously rather than thinking that our only methodology of stopping this nutty clique from getting a nuclear weapon is to have a military operation against North Korea.

Mr. YOHO. I agree.

Mr. ROHRABACHER. That would be terrible, and that should be averted if we can at all costs, which means, let's go to the strategy you have outlined today, which is a serious economic strategy to bring down and to de-place the North Korean regime that oppresses the North Korean people.

Mr. YOHO. Thank you for your comments. We will go to Dr. Ami Bera from California.

Mr. BERA. Thank you, Mr. Chairman.

I am just going to go through a series of questions, but a starting point, I think you all agree, if I am listening to your answers ask your opening testimony, at this juncture, North Korea is not going to back down and become nonnuclear. They see this as their only negotiating leverage. Would that be an accurate statement? So we don't see voluntarily stepping back; probably the exact opposite.

55

In addition, if we are not going to go to a kinetic denuclearization, which none of us think would be very easy, that means a commitment to the region, a commitment to deterrence, making sure all options obviously are on the table, but making sure our allies in the region are fully secure in our commitment. Would that be an accurate next step? And that would be exercises, that would be deployment of THAAD, and other assets that would send a strong message to North Korea that any military intervention, an errant missile going into Seoul or Tokyo would lead to dramatic repercussions. Is that accurate?

Mr. KLINGNER. Yes. We hope that more vigorous enforcement of our laws and stronger sanctions, combined with the offer of engagement if they were to do so in a pragmatic sense, would alter their behavior, but of course we need to strengthen our defenses and those of our allies, including missile defense both here in the continental U.S. as well as with our allies.

Mr. BERA. So that would be a certain next step, that deterrence, to say, it is not in your interest, North Korea, of taking provocative action.

Obviously there was some campaign trail rhetoric about South Korea or Japan pursuing nuclear options. That is not in our interest, nor do we want to start a nuclear arms race in East Asia. You know, obviously, our commitment is to that. Would that be accurate? I think South Korea pursuing nuclear weapons or Japan pursuing nuclear weapons would be not in our interests. Would you—Mr.——

Mr. LEE. With every North Korean provocation, nuclear test, the public opinion in South Korea, admittedly emotional as it may be as a snapshot of indignation of North Korea's nuclear tests, supports South Korea going nuclear. We know South Korea has the technical capability within a few months or a year to go nuclear. And in the past, of course, South Korea attempted just that under President Park Chung-hee in the early 1970s.

So although it is unlikely that South Korea will move in that direction in the foreseeable future, I think one should not be surprised if, say, 10 years from now, South Korea does make that determination at the risk of irritating or poor relations with its treaty ally, the United States, because the truth is, in the past when Britain, France, Israel went nuclear, what did the United States do? Abandon its allies and friends? No.

Mr. BERA. Sure. The danger there is when China potentially steps up their nuclear proliferation as well.

So you have given us a few tools that we could pursue. You know, let's increase sanctions, let's look at secondary sanctions, let's obviously increase our commitment to the region through military exercises, et cetera, get to the point where Kim Jong Un has to make that political calculation that the instability and his political survival is such that it is better to come to the table. Would that be an accurate assessment of some of the tools that we ought to be using?

Mr. RUGGIERO. Sure. I think that is the ultimate goal, is to increase sanctions, I would say, on North Korea and China, to try and get North Korea back to the negotiating table. But we should not kid ourselves that it is going to be easy. I would also say on the South Korea and Japan developing nuclear weapons, certainly not in our interests now, but we have to have that conversation with China. And as Dr. Lee said, that in 10 years, that calculus may change for us.

Mr. BERA. So that is also a negotiating leverage, that China needs to understand that if North Korea continues on its current path, then it may have more nuclear-armed nations in its neighborhood, which the Chinese obviously don't want. So it is in China's interest to also step up to the table.

Mr. Klingner.

Mr. KLINGNER. I think on South Korea or Japan going nuclear, while it goes against U.S. nonproliferation policy for decades, it would undermine the Nonproliferation Treaty, it could subject our allies to international sanctions themselves. But if nothing else, it would also require them to divert a large amount of their defense budget away from what they should be spending on toward duplicating a system that the U.S. is already providing with our extended deterrence guarantee.

Mr. BERA. All right. Thanks.

Mr. YOHO. Thank you, sir.

We will go to Mrs. Ann Wagner from Missouri. Thank you.

Mrs. WAGNER. Thank you, Mr. Chairman.

China is punishing South Korea economically for its decision about THAAD's deployment, but it looks like only to the extent that these actions wouldn't constitute WTO violations and that South Korea won't have any recourse mechanisms.

Mr. Klingner, do you believe China has gotten—how should I put this—smarter in how it applies economic pressures? And if over the course of the next year, if THAAD becomes a permanent reality, do you believe China will back off?

Mr. KLINGNER. I believe South Korea is going to the WTO, or is considering taking China to the WTO for its actions. China has certainly been very heavyhanded in its, really, economic attacks on South Korea. They are far more strong in their actions against South Korea's defensive moves than North Korea's offensive moves. You know, eventually, one would hope that China would realize how counterproductive their action is. The South Korean public opinion of China has plummeted. It may lead South Korea to try to diversify its economic engagement elsewhere, away from China. They have seen the actions that China has taken in the past against Japan over the Senkakus Island conflict disagreement, the belligerent actions China has taken in the South China Sea against southeast Asian nations. It can lead to all of those nations seeing that China is not a reliable partner and that they should reduce their engagement with China.

Mrs. WAGNER. And if THAAD becomes a permanent reality, you do not see China backing off?

Mr. KLINGNER. Well, we have seen China back off in its intimidation against Japan after the Senkakus incidents in 2010 and 2012, where they resumed exports of rare Earth minerals, they stopped the kind of government-induced protests against Japanese businesses. So I would hope, and I would think it would be the case, once THAAD becomes a permanent presence there, then they would realize the game is over. Also, with the likelihood of a progressive President in South Korea, who would normally be more, you know, inclined to reach out to China and North Korea, if China continues that kind of behavior, it may induce even a progressive government to not lean toward China.

Mrs. WAGNER. Thank you, Mr. Klingner.

Mr. Ruggiero, major Chinese banks have limited their exposure to North Korea, at least on the surface, I will say. But North Korean firms have successfully used Chinese middlemen and Southeast Asia and Hong Kong commercial hubs to improve procurement. Given North Korea's ability to outmaneuver current sanctions, how effective would secondary sanctions on Chinese institutions be in curbing North Korea's missile and nuclear programs?

Mr. RUGGIERO. Sure. You know, North Korea is very deceptive in its sanctions evasion activities, but the banks are responsible to ask the right questions. I would just give you one stat. In the company that we are talking about from September 2016, before the North Korean bank was designated, it did U.S. dollar transactions of $1.3 million, and afterwards, for 6 years afterwards, $110 million. So you are seeing a significant increase.

That should have caused the Chinese bank to ask questions. The Chinese bank could have investigated that company and learned that it—it showed itself as, or promoted itself as key to China-North Korea trade. So that Chinese banks should have been asking questions of why are they engaged in these transactions with North Korea.

Mrs. WAGNER. Here is an interesting question. We know that Chinese—and, again, for Mr. Ruggiero. We know that the Chinese Government has lost access to the regime's inner circle since the execution of Jang Song-thaek, Kim Jong-un's uncle. Do we know how China is mediating its lack of access to Kim Jong-un?

Mr. RUGGIERO. Well, they have stated publicly that they believe they have no levers or no way to convince North Korea to do what we essentially want them to do. And I guess my argument is that we can talk here about how do we get North Korea to change its policy, but I think we equally have to talk about how China needs to change its policy. And the way to do that is to go after their companies and banks that are allowing North Korea to do these activities.

Mrs. WAGNER. Thank you. I have many more questions, Mr. Chairman, but I will yield back my time, and I shall submit them in writing. Thank you so much.

Mr. YOHO. Great questions. And I appreciate it.

We will go to Mr. Gerry Connolly from Virginia.

Mr. CONNOLLY. Thank you.

And I am going to ask as many questions as I can, and urge you all to be concise. But thank you for being here.

Mr. Klingner, you were talking earlier about the development of a nuclear capability in the north. How realistic is that threat, though? I mean, the Korean Peninsula is pretty intimate. And, you know, even in the nonnuclear sense, the north has artillery range to Seoul. So isn't it the case that the detonation of a nuclear device of any magnitude would also adversely affect the north?

Mr. KLINGNER. Yes. But they certainly have been pursuing it for years. We think the Nodong medium-range ballistic missile is already nuclear capable, that they can already range South Korea and Japan with nuclear weapons today. We think they have perhaps 5,000 tons of chemical agent, both pervasive and nonpervasive.

Mr. CONNOLLY. Right. I get all that. My question, how real is the threat of actual utilization of such a weapon on the Korean Peninsula itself given the proximity of the north and south to each other?

Mr. KLINGNER. I think it is the threat that they hope not to use. But there is sort of a famous story that Kim Il-sung, the grandfather, asked his generals, including Kim Jong-il, of, you know, what would we do if we were losing a war? And the generals all said, we would never lose. But Kim Jong-il said, what would be the worth of the world without North Korea? So they may do a Twilight of the Gods, use it in a last ditch pulling the temple down upon themselves.

Mr. CONNOLLY. Got it.

Mr. Ruggiero, how much leverage does the United States have with respect to sanctions that we haven't deployed over North Korea? Because we don't have trade relations. We don't have economic relations. We don't directly bank with them or invest in them. I mean, what are the levers here we can use? It seems to me they are pretty limited.

Mr. RUGGIERO. Well, the U.N. Report noted, and others have noted, that North Korea needs U.S. dollars. And they need euros as well.

Mr. CONNOLLY. Right. But there are lots of ways of getting both.

Mr. RUGGIERO. Well, the ways they are doing it currently is through the American financial system. So that is a leverage point there.

The second one I would say is that while the law that was passed by this committee and signed last year was useful, and nearly doubled the number of designations over the last year, 88 percent of those are inside North Korea. That is not the way to get at the international business of North Korea.

So if you are asking about leverage, it goes back to an earlier question, the way you get at North Korea is maybe not at getting at their cognac or other parts, which is important, but focusing on the international business that North Korea——

Mr. CONNOLLY. For the record, cognac would be one thing. Mr. Sherman was talking about Johnnie Walker Black Label. Cognac, now you are talking serious.

Let me ask the same question about China. And I heard your testimony. We will stipulate what the Chinese say. But how much leverage do they have? Now, they just said that they are going to cease the purchase of coal exports from the north, which presumably is something pretty injurious to their economy. What other levers do they have they are not using?

Mr. RUGGIERO. So I would say on the coal ban, I would point out that they had a similar ban in April of last year, and after that point, they imported $800 million worth of North Korean coal. So whether or not they abide by the ban is still up for a decision. I would also go back to the Iran example, which what we saw was European banks and European companies, mostly banks, that abided by the U.S. decision to say you want to do business with Iran, you may lose your access to the United States. And that happened before European Governments came to that same decision. That is the attitude we have to have with China.

Mr. CONNOLLY. Do you believe a robust diplomatic effort by the United States is still called for and could still be efficacious?

Mr. RUGGIERO. At this time, the North Koreans say they are not interested in it. But I would say that it could be down the road after robust sanctions implementation. I think accepting a freeze at this time would just put their program in place and have the United States accepting their program as a nuclear weapons state.

Mr. CONNOLLY. Presumably, when and if that diplomatic effort needs to be launched, a planned 31 percent cut in the State Department and USAID's budget would not really be helpful.

Mr. RUGGIERO. Well, I think the diplomats at the State Department are more than capable of negotiating a deal with North Korea if they are ready to do so.

Mr. CONNOLLY. Not if there are 31 percent fewer of them. You don't have to answer.

I yield back.

Mr. YOHO. Thank you, sir, for your questions, as always.

We are going to go back to Mr. Sherman for another round, if you guys are up to it. If so, we sure would appreciate it.

Mr. SHERMAN. I want to build on Gerry's comment about the need for a robust State Department. We may be able, no matter how big the State Department is, to send five diplomats or ten diplomats to Six-Party Talks or any kind of talks. But if we want sanctions, that means going to every country and trying to get them to change the behavior of their bank, their distillery, or I guess if you want cognac, maybe some other kind. That is incredibly labor-intensive. It is company by company, country by country.

Mr. CONNOLLY. And that takes a skill set, does it not, Mr. Sherman?

Mr. SHERMAN. Yes, it does. But I want to focus on, we saw the assassination of Kim Jong Nam. It happened to happen recently. Is that because there was a unique opportunity because of his travel outside China? Or is that because of a unique or increased level of desire by the Pyongyang regime to assassinate him? Was he uniquely vulnerable when he was assassinated or was there a change in North Korean policy? Dr. Lee, do you have a view?

Mr. LEE. I think the timing of it is significant. In 1997, the day before Kim Jong-il's birthday, which is February 16, on the 15th of February, 1997, Kim Jong-il's nephew was assassinated in South Korea. Why? Because he had defected and written an expose on the royal family. And I believe that was sort of a birthday gift to the so-called Dear Leader by his agents, to kill him on the eve of Kim Jong-il's birthday.

Mr. SHERMAN. But has North Korea been trying pretty hard to kill this uncle every day of the week or did they——

Mr. LEE. The half-brother.

Mr. SHERMAN. The half-brother, excuse me.

Mr. LEE. Well, I think the half-brother, Kim Jong-nam, was vulnerable. North Korean agents clearly would have access to his travel itinerary. But I think they saw it as the best time to do it, to carry out the act on the day of his return to China. I think they would have been reticent to do something like this on Chinese territory. That is why it was in Malaysia.

Mr. SHERMAN. Did he travel often outside of China?

Mr. LEE. Yes, sir, he did.

Mr. SHERMAN. So they had other non-Chinese opportunities.

I don't know which of you is most qualified to answer this. But what are the estimated hard currency and gold reserves of the North Korean Government? Anybody have a guess? Dr. Lee?

Mr. LEE. I am just a newspaper reader, but for years, there have been newspaper reports of $1 billion to $4 billion or $5 billion in offshore secret accounts in Europe and in China.

Mr. SHERMAN. So they trust the international banking system, or at least they are partners in it. It is not like they have the currency or the gold in Pyongyang itself. They are relying on bank accounts.

Mr. LEE. Well, according to the U.N. Panel of Experts report, most of North Korea's international financial transactions were denominated in the U.S. dollar from foreign-based banks, transferred through corresponding accounts in the United States.

Mr. SHERMAN. But their reserves they are willing to deposit with foreign-based banks rather than under their mattress?

Mr. LEE. I think that gives us leverage.

Mr. SHERMAN. It does, and I am surprised they are willing to do that.

How much does North Korea earn from the export of coal or anything else that they can actually export from their own territory? And how does that compare to how much they generate by exporting labor, whether it be, you know, the workers that they have sent abroad? Can we put these two sources of foreign income in perspective?

Mr. KLINGNER. That is a very good question, sir. I think the most prevalent estimates of the overseas labor is $200 million to $300 million a year. The coal, I think the limit on it was going to reduce North Korean income by $800 million a year.

Mr. RUGGIERO. Last year it was $1.2 billion.

Mr. SHERMAN. One point two billion in coal. Do they export anything else other than coal from their territory that is worth talking about?

Mr. KLINGNER. Other resources. Resources are a large part of their exports.

Mr. SHERMAN. And so in addition to the coal, any idea what the other resources generate?

Mr. KLINGNER. Some of the resources, minerals, have been precluded from export by the U.N. resolution.

Mr. SHERMAN. How willing is North Korea to sell a nuclear bomb? How many nuclear weapons would they have to have for their own use before they would think, well, this one might be extra? Or at least something that we would sell if we could get a really good deal? I will ask Dr. Lee first.

Mr. LEE. I think the risk is plausible. It is high, actually. We know North Korea has sold arms to terrorist organizations. We know North Korea has built a nuclear reactor in Syria, which the Israelis took out in September 2007. North Korea is one of the world's——

Mr. SHERMAN. Are they to the point where, under their own military strategy, they are close to having an "extra or not absolutely essential nuclear device," or do they need all the ones they can produce this year for their own defense strategy?

Mr. LEE. Well, experts vary on what a second strike capability is, perhaps 40 or 50 bombs. Some people estimate that North Korea is very close to having 20 right now. And this will be accelerated in the years to come, their capability.

Mr. SHERMAN. So you think they would want 40 for their own defense strategy before they might be willing to sell missile material. Though, of course, they have already shown the last decade a willingness to sell a technology kit, if you will, that was destroyed in Syria. Do you have any comment?

Mr. RUGGIERO. I would just say I think they are far more likely to try and milk any nuclear technology in terms of the amount of money they can get. So they are far more likely to duplicate what they did in Syria. So selling the means to be able to produce missile material. I think North Korea values their nuclear weapons. I don't think they will actually sell a device. But they are more than willing to sell UF6, like reportedly they sold to Libya.

Mr. SHERMAN. UF6?

Mr. RUGGIERO. I am sorry, the material they used for centrifuges.

Mr. SHERMAN. So they will sell technology, equipment that can be used to refine uranium or otherwise meld a nuclear weapon.

Mr. RUGGIERO. My point is there is more money—I mean, obviously they would get a lot of money if they sold one weapon. But they can get more money, like their ballistic missile program, if countries or other groups are interested in the full nuclear cycle.

Mr. SHERMAN. While the chairman is being indulgent, I will also ask you, is this regime so vulnerable that a 20 percent decline, 30 percent decline in the hard currency that they spend on their elites could actually be regime-endangering? This is back to the Johnnie Walker question.

Mr. RUGGIERO. Right. So I think we have examples in the past, Banco Delta Asia in 2005 and other examples, that if we find the right levers that North Korea is very interested in, whether it is Johnnie Walker or——

Mr. SHERMAN. Yeah, we can make them mad. I know that. Can we endanger the regime?

Mr. RUGGIERO. I think there is a way to get them to change their calculus. Whether we can get the Chinese on board for changing the regime, that would be the question.

Mr. SHERMAN. Well, you may not quite change the regime, but until you are regime endangering, they are not going to give up the crown jewels.

I will yield back.

Mr. YOHO. I appreciate it. And those were great questions.

If you will indulge me for a few more minutes. Again, if I look back over history, I was born in 1955, North Korea I think started around 1945. I am 62, so they are 72 years old. Has anybody tried to invade them in 72 years?

I look from my standpoint where I am, as a Member of Congress, as a United States citizen, they don't have anything really that I want. I would think they should know that, that in 72 years, no-body has really tried to invade them. They invaded the south. I would hope that the rest of the world would look at the threat that they pose getting a nuclear weapon, and the irresponsibility that we have seen with the VX nerve agent that we know, the stockpile, with the VX murder of his half-brother, and with the other mur-ders that we have seen using the poison needles. Is there anybody else in the world kind of concerned about this outside of the Asia-Pacific theater of South Korea and Japan?

Mr. KLINGNER. Well, I think in the last year particularly, we have seen a growing international willingness to work against North Korea. One would have thought it would have been done after the first three nuclear tests, but it took the fourth test. And so what we have seen is a new willingness, not only on the sanc-tions and the targeted financial measures, but also going after even legitimate North Korean businesses. And it is a way of tightening the economic noose.

So as we have tried to finally get stronger, more robust imple-mentation of our laws and the resolutions, which is still lagging, but also South Korea and others have gone around the world talk-ing to their legitimate business partners saying, do you really want to be doing business with someone who is involved in slave labor, crimes against humanity, and now using a chemical weapon of mass destruction in a civilian airport? We can try to wean away North Korea's business partners.

Mr. YOHO. Yeah, that is pretty bold, when you do that in a public space like that with a toxic substance that is the most lethal nerve gas that we know.

Mr. SHERMAN. If I can interject, and holding Malaysians hostage in their country.

Mr. YOHO. Right. So I guess what I am trying to get out of you is how do you involve the rest of the world? Like, this is a serious problem. Obviously, they don't see it as serious as we do, or maybe Japan or South Korea, that we need to get the buy-in for the sanc-tions to work. How do you go to the U.N. and say we need world cooperation? Because this is not good for anybody, not just the re-gion, but it would upset the whole applecart of the world, not just trade, but, you know, stability around the world.

How do you get the rest of the world to buy into that and say we need you at the table to do this? Is this something we can put pressure on through our U.N. partners and just say, you know what, we cut off funds until you come to the table and—I am at a loss here, because I find it very disturbing that not everybody is standing behind us saying let's go, let's put these sanctions on and bring this regime—I don't want to say to an end, but bring the de-structive nature of what they are doing to an end.

Dr. Lee, what is your thoughts on how we accomplish that?

Mr. LEE. I believe the United States is in a unique position, uniquely well positioned to take that leadership role to make the point that tougher sanctions are necessary.

Mr. YOHO. Where would you do that? At the U.N.?

Mr. LEE. Well, through the respective U.S. Embassies in those nations. Give other nations the choice.

Mr. YOHO. Is it an ultimatum?

Mr. LEE. No. Trading with North Korea or with us. No one is calling for an all-out trade war with China, but U.S. sanctions against North Korea have been very, very weak, both in degree and kind.

Mr. YOHO. And we are at a point where we can't afford to be weak.

Mr. LEE. There is no need to be weak, in my view.

Mr. YOHO. I agree.

Mr. LEE. The self-restraint exercise over the past 70 years with each North Korean lethal provocation probably has contributed to the de facto peace in the region, but we have spoiled North Korea.

Mr. YOHO. Mr. Ruggiero, I am going to go to you and just ask, in addition to the sanctions following the reinstatement of the North Korean State Sponsor of Terrorism, Thae Yong-ho was noted as saying that the best thing that we can do—who is the highest ranking North Korean defector in decades—recently said that this was the best way to force change in North Korea by injecting outside information. And I don't look at it as propaganda. I look at it as injecting truth to the North Korean people. Because you have got a society for 70 years who has only known repression. They don't know what it is outside. And my wife and I watched a video the other day of the young girl that came through China and told a very compelling story that would bring tears to anybody's eyes.

How do you get that story into North Korea? What is the best way? Is it through the SIM cards, through broadcasting? All of the above? Leaflets? I would like to hear your thoughts on that.

Mr. RUGGIERO. Well, I think all of the above is the right approach. I think there was a report earlier this week that North Korea had sent leaflets to South Korea talking about its own ballistic missile program. And so, you know, I think we should be meeting back and forth with leaflets. I think you said SIM cards. I know USB drives are another area that has been looked at.

I would also, if you don't mind on the prior question, that is why I would go back to the Iran sanctions model. The attitude there was to go to all these countries. And I would just say that, you know, I know the SWIFT financial messaging was a small amount, but the fact that Belgium thought it was a good idea to allow SWIFT to conduct transactions with U.N.-designated banks just shows you the attitude and the problem that we have. I wouldn't go through the U.N.

Mr. YOHO. I don't understand how they did that or why they did that.

Mr. RUGGIERO. I don't either. I have written about how it is probably a violation of U.S.—excuse me, the POE, the Panel of Experts, has said it was a U.N. violation. The U.N.-designated banks using the service was probably a violation of the law that was passed last year. I think things like that are areas where we need to be increasing our efforts, our implementation efforts.

Mr. YOHO. All right. One final comment from my friend from California.

Mr. SHERMAN. I certainly agree on an all-out effort on information, an all-out effort on the sanctions regime that we have. But when you hold up the Iran model, keep in mind, that was a much more vulnerable country because it has to provide a higher standard of living to its people and because it doesn't have China in its corner. And in spite of that, we were only able to extract rather modest limits on its nuclear program. We are trying to do far more with regard to North Korea.

And I yield back.

Mr. YOHO. Thank you, sir. And I would like to thank my ranking member and my colleague, Mr. Sherman, as well as all the other members that were here too, to ask questions. And I would like to thank the witnesses for coming to share their expertise on this important hearing and this important issue.

This meeting is adjourned. And thank you guys for your time.

[Whereupon, at 2:33 p.m., the subcommittee was adjourned.]

A P P E N D I X

Material Submitted for the Record

SUBCOMMITTEE HEARING NOTICE
COMMITTEE ON FOREIGN AFFAIRS
U.S. HOUSE OF REPRESENTATIVES
WASHINGTON, DC 20515-6128

Subcommittee on Asia and the Pacific
Ted Yoho (R-FL), Chairman

March 21, 2017

TO: MEMBERS OF THE COMMITTEE ON FOREIGN AFFAIRS

You are respectfully requested to attend an OPEN hearing of the Committee on Foreign Affairs, to be held by the Subcommittee on Asia and the Pacific in Room 2172 of the Rayburn House Office Building (and available live on the Committee website at http://www.ForeignAffairs.house.gov):

DATE: Tuesday, March 21, 2017

TIME: 2:00 p.m.

SUBJECT: Pressuring North Korea: Evaluating Options

WITNESSES: Mr. Bruce Klingner
                 Senior Research Fellow for Northeast Asia
                 The Heritage Foundation

                 Sung-Yoon Lee, Ph.D.
                 Kim Koo-Korea Foundation Professor in Korean Studies and Assistant Professor
                 The Fletcher School of Law and Diplomacy
                 Tufts University

                 Mr. Anthony Ruggiero
                 Senior Fellow
                 Foundation for Defense of Democracies

By Direction of the Chairman

The Committee on Foreign Affairs seeks to make its facilities accessible to persons with disabilities. If you are in need of special accommodations, please call 202/225-5021 at least four business days in advance of the event, whenever practicable. Questions with regard to special accommodations in general (including availability of Committee materials in alternative formats and assistive listening devices) may be directed to the Committee.

COMMITTEE ON FOREIGN AFFAIRS

MINUTES OF SUBCOMMITTEE ON _____ *Asia and the Pacific* _____ HEARING

Day _*Tuesday*_ Date _*03.21.2017*_ Room _*2172 RHOB*_

Starting Time _*2:06 pm*_ Ending Time _*3:32 pm*_

Recesses _____ (____ to ____) (____ to ____) (____ to ____) (____ to ____) (____ to ____) (____ to ____)

Presiding Member(s)
Chairman Ted Yoho (R-FL)

Check all of the following that apply:

Open Session ☑
Executive (closed) Session ☐
Televised ☐

Electronically Recorded (taped) ☐
Stenographic Record ☐

TITLE OF HEARING:
"Pressuring North Korea: Evaluating Options"

SUBCOMMITTEE MEMBERS PRESENT:
Rep. Ted Yoho, Rep. Dana Rohrabacher, Rep. Steve Chabot, Rep. Ann Wagner
Rep. Brad Sherman, Rep. Ami Bera, Rep. Tulsi Gabbard, Rep. Dina Titus, Rep. Gerald Connolly

NON-SUBCOMMITTEE MEMBERS PRESENT: *(Mark with an * if they are not members of full committee.)*
N/A

HEARING WITNESSES: Same as meeting notice attached? Yes ☑ No ☐
(If "no", please list below and include title, agency, department, or organization.)

STATEMENTS FOR THE RECORD: *(List any statements submitted for the record.)*
Rep. Gerald Connolly

TIME SCHEDULED TO RECONVENE _____
or
TIME ADJOURNED _____

Subcommittee Staff Associate

Statement for the Record

Congressman Gerald Connolly
AP Subcommittee Hearing: "Pressuring North Korea: Evaluating Options"
March 21, 2017

It is undeniable that North Korea's nuclear and ballistic missile programs have accelerated in recent years. North Korea conducted two nuclear tests and more than 20 missile tests in 2016 alone. During the most recent test on March 6, 2017, the regime simultaneously launched four intermediate-range ballistic missiles towards the Sea of Japan. Three of these missiles landed within 200 nautical miles of Japan's coastline, inside its exclusive economic zone (EEZ).

President Trump and his administration must get serious about this threat. The President has the necessary authorities to levy sanctions against North Korea and its weapons programs, and Congress appears willing to authorize additional sanctions this Session. Last year, Congress passed H.R. 757, the North Korea Sanctions and Policy Enhancement Act, which strengthens sanctions against North Korea in response to its continued efforts to build a nuclear arsenal. That bill included two of my amendments: one conditioning sanctions relief on the promotion of family reunifications for Koreans and Korean Americans, and another to ensure that U.S. policy toward North Korea is informed by the recommendations made in the United Nations' commission of Inquiry on Human Rights in North Korea. It is vital that our North Korea policy be informed with an understanding that there are human victims of the ongoing conflict on the Peninsula.

In response to North Korea's fourth nuclear test in January 2016, the United States helped negotiate the passage of United Nations Security Council (UNSC) Resolution 2270. This hard-fought measure imposed sweeping new sectoral and banking sanctions on Pyongyang and required states to strengthen interdiction efforts against North Korea's illicit proliferation and trade networks. Following North Korea's fifth nuclear test in September 2016, the UNSC passed Resolution 2321, which strengthened the U.N. sanctions regime against the DPRK by enacting further export restrictions and limitations on official government bank accounts. Even though China agreed to both UNSC 2270 and 2321, enforcement against Chinese companies doing business with North Korea has not been robust. For example, the Chinese government provides a form letter that companies seeking to claim a "livelihood" exemption can copy, paste, and submit if they would like to continue to conduct trade with North Korea.

The crux of the problem does not lie with existing sanctions authority, but rather with the lack of Chinese enforcement. If the United States wants to make any meaningful progress toward halting North Korea's nuclear and ballistic missile programs, the Trump Administration must demonstrate to China it is in their best interest to enforce existing sanctions against North Korea. However, the Trump Administration's barrage of contradictory signals toward China complicates such an effort. Whether President Trump is flirting with the notion of rejecting the

"One China" policy or threatening to launch a trade war with the Chinese, his inflammatory remarks do not set the stage for effective diplomacy.

We turn to diplomacy to solve our most intractable national security challenges, including the conflict on the Peninsula. Pulling out the rug beneath our nation's diplomats, as the President's FY 2018 budget request does, undermines and further exposes our military by shifting the entire burden to the Department of Defense. We cannot starve our diplomacy and foreign aid missions and expect that increased defense spending alone will keep America safe. Secretary of Defense James Mattis himself has said: "If you don't fund the State Department fully, then I need to buy more ammunition." This conflict does not need more ammunition.

The Korean Peninsula remains one of the most dangerous flashpoints on the globe. Navigating this complex web of regional stakeholders and competing interests will require patient and committed U.S. leadership to avert the ever-present potential of conflict that looms over 75 million Koreans. I look forward to hearing from our witnesses today regarding how best to achieve that goal and halt the North Korean regime's dangerous provocations.

www.ingramcontent.com/pod-product-compliance
Lightning Source LLC
Chambersburg PA
CBHW081413280526
45788CB00009B/3079